CHRISTMAS RECIPES

Best Vegetarian Christmas Cookbook for Dummies

(Holiday Casserole Recipes for a Wonderful, Stress-free Christmas)

Christopher Demaio

Published by Alex Howard

© **Christopher Demaio**

All Rights Reserved

Christmas Recipes: Best Vegetarian Christmas Cookbook for Dummies (Holiday Casserole Recipes for a Wonderful, Stress-free Christmas)

ISBN 978-1-989891-99-5

All rights reserved. No part of this guide may be reproduced in any form without permission in writing from the publisher except in the case of brief quotations embodied in critical articles or reviews.

Legal & Disclaimer

The information contained in this book is not designed to replace or take the place of any form of medicine or professional medical advice. The information in this book has been provided for educational and entertainment purposes only.

The information contained in this book has been compiled from sources deemed reliable, and it is accurate to the best of the Author's knowledge; however, the Author cannot guarantee its accuracy and validity and cannot be held liable for any errors or omissions. Changes are periodically made to this book. You must consult your doctor or get professional medical advice before using any of the suggested remedies, techniques, or information in this book.

Table of contents

PART 1 1

INTRODUCTION 2

APPETIZERS 3

    Avocado and Cranberry Salsa 3
    Balls of Cheese 5
    Cheese Covered with Pistachio Layer 7
    Cornmeal Squares with Gorgonzola and Almonds 9
    Creamy Pumpkin Soup 11
    Gingered Nuts with Sesame Seeds 13
    Onion Dip 15
    Pecans Baked Brie 17
    Tiny Bread Dough Basket Filled Smoked Salmon Salad 19
    Walnut and Blue Cheese Dip 21

MAIN DISHES 22

    Baked Ham with Cola 22
    Cornish Hens with Honey and Poppy Seeds 23
    Meatloaf for Thanksgiving 24
    Navy Style Roasted Turkey 25
    Orange Duck 27
    Perfectly Roasted Turkey 29
    Roasted Apple Cider Turkey 31
    Roasted Turkey with Herbs 33
    Simple Turkey in a Bag 35
    Smoked Turkey 36
    Stuffed Pumpkin 38
    Stuffed Pumpkin II 40
    Super Turkey 42
    Thanksgiving Turkey Prepared in Slow Cooker 44
    Turkey Legs prepared in Slow Cooker 46

SIDE DISHES 47

    Bananas and Honey with Whipped Sweet Potatoes 47
    Butternut Squash Macaroni and Cheese 49

Corn and Pumpkin Bread 51
Cranberry Sauce with Honey 53
Green Bean and Mushroom Casserole 55
Mashed Potatoes gently baked and prepared with Parmesan Cheese and Bread Crumbs 57
Mashed Potatoes prepared with Sour Cream and Chive 59
Mashed Potatoes with Truffles and Cheese 61
Mushroom and Broccoli with Cheese 63
Quick Rolls 65
Roasted Cauliflower with Butter and Garlic 67
Roasted Sweet Potatoes with Honey and Cinnamon 69
Soft Sweet Corn Bread 70
Tricolor Mashed Potatoes 72

DESSERTS 74

Apple Cider Apple Pie 74
Butter and Milk Pie 77
Cocoa Cream Pie 79
Lime Pie with Coconut 80
Orange and Cranberry Gelatin 82
Peanut Butter and Vanilla Fudge 84
Pecan Pie 85
Pumpkin and Hazelnut Pie 88
Pumpkin Pudding 90
Two-layer Pumpkin Pie 91
Vanilla and Carrot Soufflé 93

PART 2 94

CHAPTER 1: CANAPÉS AND SALADS 95

(1) Marinated Eel - Anguilla Marinata 95
(2) Clams Casino 98
(3) Seven Fishes Seafood Salad 101
(4) Anchovies in a Lemon Marinade - Acciughe al Limone 105
(5) Salmon Canapés 107
(6) Baby Octopus Salad 109
(7) Tuna Canapés - Tartine al Tonno 111

(8) SHRIMP COCKTAIL - COCKTAIL DI GAMBERETTI 113
(9) ITALIAN SEAFOOD SALAD – INSALATA DI MARE 115
(10) ITALIAN SALT COD SALAD - INSALATA DI BACCALÀ 117

CHAPTER 2: ROASTED, FRIED AND HEARTY 119

(11) WHOLE-ROASTED FENNEL AND ONION BRANZINO 119
(12) CRUMB-TOPPED BAKED CLAMS – VONGOLE AL FORNO 121
(13) SLOW ROASTED SALMON IN LEMON OIL 123
(14) FRITTO MISTO 125
(15) SEARED SCALLOPS WITH HERBY CITRUS SAUCE 127
(16) HOUSEWIFE STYLE JUMBO SHRIMP MARSALA - GAMBERONI ALLA CASALINGA SICILIANA 129
(17) SEAFOOD STUFFED SALMON FILLETS 131
(18) OVEN ROASTED BACCALA WITH POTATOES 133
(19) SEA BASS ALLA FIORENTINA 135
(20) SAUTÉED SOLE WITH OLIVE TAPENADE 137

CHAPTER 3: PASTA AND STEW 139

(21) UMBRIAN FISH STEW 139
(22) LINGUINE WITH TUNA PUTTANESCA 142
(23) TUSCAN SEAFOOD STEW – CACCIUCCO 145
(24) LOBSTER FRA DIAVOLO 148
(25) SQUID INK SEAFOOD PASTA 151
(26) NONNA'S CIOPPINO 153
(27) SPAGHETTI WITH CLAMS - SPAGHETTI ALLE VONGOLE 156
(28) SALTED COD - BACCALA STEW 159
(29) SPAGHETTI WITH ANCHOVIES - SPAGHETTI CON ACCIUGHE 162
(30) SEA BASS & SEAFOOD ITALIAN ONE-POT 164

CHAPTER 4: PALETTE CLEANSERS AND DESSERTS 166

(31) SPARKLING PROSECCO SGROPPINO 166
(32) AFTER-DINNER BISCOTTI 167
(33) RED GRAPEFRUIT AND BLACK PEPPER SORBETTO 170
(34) CHOCOLATE COVERED ITALIAN FLAG COOKIES 171
(35) PIZZELLE DELLA NONNA 175
(36) CHRISTMAS FRIED HONEY FRITTERS – STRUFFOLI 177
(37) LIMONCELLO GELATO 179

(38) CANDIED CHRISTMAS SEMIFREDDO WITH CHERRY LIQUEUR FRUITCAKE 181

(39) DRIED CRANBERRY, PISTACHIO, AND GINGER CANNOLI 183

(40) DOUBLE CHOCOLATE RUM STUFFED PANETTONE - PANETTONE RIPIENO AL DOPPIO CIOCCOLATO 185

APPETIZERS 187

TOMATO-MOZZARELLA BITES 187

STUFFED MUSHROOMS 188

HOMEMADE SALSA 189

SNACKS 190

CHEESE AND CRACKERS PLATTER 191

Part 1

Introduction

Reunite with your family and friends this Thanksgiving to give thanks for all the valuable things we have. Thanksgiving has always been a great opportunity to share a special dinner with our loved ones. This recipe book invites you to try to kindle the real meaning of thanksgiving by creating food so delicious that all who have a bite will be more grateful about your food than anything else!

There's a recipe inside for everyone! Discover the tasty dishes that will be talked about for long after Thanksgiving. You'll find appetizers, main dishes, side dishes, and desserts. There's a recipe inside for everyone. If you don't like turkey, try some duck! If you don't like duck, try some meatloaf! Don't feel like eating pie? Have some pudding instead.

All of the recipes are guaranteed to be simple, and easy to prepare, but at the same time, so full of love, flavor, texture, and colors that will transform your table into a food festival that your guests will wish would last forever.

Appetizers

Avocado and Cranberry Salsa

Today we introduce you this tasty, soft, and aromatic dish; and the best of all is its easy preparation! This is definitely an excellent appetizer for thanksgiving. Yummy!

Yields: Makes 4 servings.

Ingredients
1 tablespoon lime juice, fresh
2 tablespoons honey
1 jalapeno, chopped
1/4 cup red onion, minced
2 mellow avocados cut into 1/4-inch pieces
2 tablespoons cilantro, fresh and minced
3/4 cup halved cranberries
Coarse salt
Pepper, ground
Tortilla chips

Method of preparation
1. Mix together 1 tablespoon of lime juice, 1 chopped jalapeno (remove seeds if less heat is desired), 2 tablespoons honey, and 1/4 cup minced red onion in a large bowl.

2. Add the 1/4-inch pieces of 2 mellow avocados, 3/4 cup halve cranberries; use paper towels to drain well, and 2 tablespoons minced cilantro.
3. Add coarse salt and pepper to season.
4. Mix smoothly to combine.

Balls of Cheese

Describing cheese may be a difficult task. Fortunately, is other way around when eating it so let's not waste out time trying to describe this recipe, which of course is full of flavor, and let's eat it instead!

Yields: Makes 16 servings.

Ingredients
1 pound cream cheese, room temperature
2 1/2 strong Cheddar cheese, delicately shredded
1 tablespoon mustard, Dijon
1 teaspoon Worcestershire sauce
Pepper, ground
1 cup pecans, delicately minced

Method of preparation
1. Beat Cheddar cheese, Dijon mustard, Worcestershire sauce, cream cheese, and an acceptable pinch of pepper with an electric mixer in a large bowl until well combined.
2. Incorporate 1/4 cup pecans.
3. Using plastic wrap, cover the cheese mixture, and cool for at least 2 1/2 hours or up to overnight.
4. Separate the cheese mixture in 2 parts, and form each half into spheres.
5. Put on a plate the remaining 3/4 cup pecans, and roll the cheese spheres on pecans making sure of

pressing against nuts to adhere until completely covered.
6. Let cool and serve.

Cheese Covered with Pistachio Layer

Tired of eating cheese by itself? Probably not, but you can add some Pistachios to incorporate more flavor into it. This recipe is tasty, but at the same time easy to prepare, that way you get to spend more time with your beloved family, and less time in the kitchen!

Yields: Makes 8 servings.

Ingredients
8 ounces of cream cheese at room temperature
4 ounces roughly shredded strong white Cheddar
1 tablespoon Dijon mustard
1 teaspoon Worcestershire sauce
Salt, coarse
Pepper, ground
1 cup with shell and unsalted pistachios, roughly minced
Crackers, for serving

Method of preparation
1. Beat the Cheddar cheese, cream cheese, Dijon mustard, Worcestershire sauce using an electric mixer in a medium bowl until well combined.
2. Add pepper and salt to season.
3. Cover and refrigerate for 1 or 2 hours until smoothly firm.
4. In another frying pan, stirring constantly, toast pistachios for 7 minutes until golden and fragrant.

5. Put in a plate and let chill.
6. Put the cheese mixture on waxed paper. Shape into 6-inch log using paper.
7. Drizzle with pistachios, and press to adhere.
8. Using a piece of waxed paper, wrap log.
9. Let cool for 1 or 2 hours (up to 1 day) until firm.
10. Serve with crackers.

Cornmeal Squares with Gorgonzola and Almonds

Before you serve that delicious turkey, enrich your guests' palate with one of these crunchy squares. Make sure to mix different flavors on the table.

Yields: Makes 10 servings.

Ingredients:
4 1/4 cups of water
1 cup of quick-cooking cornmeal
1 teaspoon of salt
Cooking spray
3 tablespoons currants
1/3 cup Gorgonzola cheese, grind
3 tablespoons almonds
1 teaspoon orange skin, grate
2/3 cup balsamic vinegar
2 tablespoons cut flat-leaf parsley

Method of preparation:
1. Put the 4 cups of water to boil in a medium saucepan.
2. Gently add the cornmeal and salt, making sure to constantly mix using a whisk.
3. Reduce heat to the lowest, and cook until soupy. Stir frequently.
4. Mix with butter.

5. Move the cornmeal into a 9-inch squared baking pan covered equally with cooking spray.
6. Cover entirely the cornmeal with plastic wrap.
7. Cool for 1 hour or until polenta is solid.
8. Divide into 30 squares.
9. Bring 1/4 cup of water to a boil, and combine it with currants in a small bowl.
10. Chill for 10 minutes or until currants swell.
11. Add the vinegar in a small saucepan and heat it.
12. Cook the vinegar at medium-low heat for approximately 10 minutes or until it has been reduced to 2 tablespoons.
13. Let it cool a little.
14. Bring a nonstick to the stove and heat it at medium-high heat.
15. Spread cooking spray all over the pan.
16. Take half of the polenta squares and put them in the pan.
17. Cook for 6 minutes on each side until golden.
18. Remove the cornmeal squares from the pan. Make sure to keep them warm.
19. Repeat the exact same steps with the other half of the cornmeal squares.
20. Cover the top of each polenta square with 1/2 teaspoon of cheese.
21. Sprinkle with 1/4 teaspoon of balsamic vinegar.
22. Decorate with parsley.

Creamy Pumpkin Soup

To all of us like to bring our family together and prepare something simple, but amazing. Though we may already have our recipes ready, we may consider cooking something new this year to surprise our guests.
This pumpkin should be one recipe to consider!

Yields: Makes 3 servings.

Ingredients:
1 small-medium pumpkin
1/4 cup of cream
1 teaspoon cinnamon, ground
1 teaspoon salt
1/4 teaspoon clove
1/2 teaspoon nutmeg
3 tablespoons sugar
1/4 teaspoon pepper, white

Method of preparation
1. Cut the top of the pumpkin and take out the seeds and the fibrous content. (Save the shell for later.)
2. Obtain as most content of the pumpkin as you can. Be careful! Don't break the shell, or make holes on it.
3. Once you've extracted the pulp, put it in a pan.
4. Mix 1/2 cup of water with sugar and cook the pulp over medium heat.

5. Chill for 10 minutes.
6. Put the pulp in a food processor, and blend until creamy.
7. Add clove and other spices.
8. Put all the ingredients (but the cream) in a big pan and bring to a boil and cook for 10 minutes. Add water if necessary (1/2 cup should be enough.)
9. Add the cream and stir well.
10. Reduce the heat to low and cook for 10 more minutes.
11. Place the soup into the pumpkin's shell and sprinkle with mozzarella cheese.

Gingered Nuts with Sesame Seeds

Something appetizing to give as an appetizer: some nuts with sesame seeds! Flavor and proteins makes this dish something flavorful and nutritious. What could be better?

Yields: Makes 16 servings.

Ingredients
3 cups unsalted mixed nuts
3/4 cup candied ginger, chopped
1/4 teaspoon cayenne pepper
2 teaspoons coarse salt
1/4 teaspoon pepper, ground
1/4 cup sugar
1/4 cup water

Method of preparation
1. Heat oven to 350 degrees Fahrenheit.
2. Combine candied ginger, nuts, cayenne pepper, pepper, salt, and sesame seeds in a large bowl.
3. Combine water and sugar in a small medium pan, and heat over medium-high.
4. Bring to a boil and cook for 3 minutes until sugar dissolves, stirring occasionally.
5. Sprinkle sugar syrup over the nut mixture and agitate mix well to combine.
6. Make a single layer arrangement on a parchment-lined rimmed baking tray.

7. Bake for 15 or 20 minutes, stirring constantly, until the nuts look golden.
8. Let chill entirely on tray on a wire rack before breaking into tiny-size parts.

Onion Dip

Onion lover? Dip lover? Imagine both flavors combined! This onion dip, for sure, be the main subject of conversation of each one of your guests during the entire night (or until you serve your delicious and flavorful turkey.)

Yields: Makes 2 cups.

Ingredients
1 tablespoon olive oil
1 pound Vidalia onions, delicately minced
1 cup sour cream, reduced-fat
2 ounces cream cheese at room temperature, reduced-fat
1 1/2 teaspoons white-wine vinegar
1/4 cup chives, delicately minced
Potato chips, for serving
Coarse salt
Pepper, ground

Method of preparation
1. Heat oil over medium in a large frying pan.
2. Incorporate the onions.
3. Add pepper and salt to season.
4. Stirring constantly, cook for 12 or 15 minutes until golden brown.
5. Let chill to room temperature.

6. Combine sour cream, cream cheese, vinegar, chives and onions in a medium bowl.
7. Let cool dip for 1 hour until lightly dense.

Pecans Baked Brie

Thanksgiving is around the corner, and it's a great excuse to come up with a family reunion to thank for all the great things in our lives, and to thank because we can finally have some Pecans with Brie Cheese as appetizer. Yummy!

Yields: Makes 8 servings.

Ingredients
1/2 cup pecans
3 tablespoons brown sugar, light
3 tablespoons maple syrup, pure
Sliced baguette or crackers, for serving
1 small rounded Brie or Camembert cheese

Method of preparation
1. Heat oven to 350 degrees.
2. Place cheese on a thin baking tray; bake for 15 to 20 minutes until softened.
3. Put on a serving tray and chill for 20 minutes.
4. Put nuts on a clean oven sheet; bake for 7 or 10 minutes until pecans are fragrant and toasted.
5. Drizzle nuts over the top of cheese.
6. Combine maple syrup and sugar in a small pot and, over medium heat, bring to a boil and simmer for 1 or 2 minutes until spumy.
7. Sprinkle warm, but lightly cold sauce over the nuts and cheese.

8. Serve with baguette or crackers.

Tiny Bread Dough Basket Filled Smoked Salmon Salad

Let's celebrate this Thanksgiving with these bread dough baskets filled with cold smoked salmon salad. This is a very simple recipe to prepare, and they will draw a smile on your guests' face. Guaranteed!

Yields: Makes 38-40 servings.

Ingredients:
2 refrigerated pie crusts.
1 cup of salmon, smoked
1/8 cup cream cheese
Juice of half lemon
2 tablespoons red onion, chopped
2 tablespoons bell pepper
2 tablespoons mayonnaise
2 tablespoons chive

Method of preparation
1. You will need a mini cupcake baking tray and one 2 1/2-inch round cutter.
2. Heat the oven to 350-Fahrenheit degrees.
3. Stretch the pie crusts and cut it into, approximately, 38-40 pieces using the round cutter.
4. Put the 38-40 pieces in the oven and bake them for 12-15 minutes.
5. Once they are ready, take them out of the oven.

6. Chill at room temperature.
7. Cut the smoked salmon into small pieces. Mix the pieces with cream cheese and the other ingredients.
8. Fill the tiny bread dough baskets and decorate with mint leafs.

Walnut and Blue Cheese Dip

What's better? Blue cheese? Walnuts? Why not both? Our polenta squares will give your meal the deserved start. You can also combine these tasty snacks with savory dried figs or blueberries.

Yields: Makes 1 1/3 cups.

Ingredients
4 ounces of cream cheese at room temperature
1/2 cup walnuts, minced
Salt, coarse
Pepper, ground
4 ounces cold minced blue cheese, such as Stilton
Crostini or crackers for serving

Method of preparation
1. Stir cream cheese in a medium bowl using a wooden spoon until tender.
2. Incorporate the walnuts.
3. Add pepper and salt to season.
4. Smoothly fold in blue cheese, disintegrating carefully.
5. Put the mixture in a small bowl; soft surface.
6. Serve with crostini or crackers.

Main Dishes

Baked Ham with Cola

Ham and Cola. Where are you going to get something more southern than this?

Yields: Makes 1 ham.

Ingredients
10 pounds ham, pre-cooked
1/2 can of a soda cola-flavored, carbonated

Method of preparation
1. Heat the oven to 275 degrees Fahrenheit.
2. Eliminate any excessive fat from ham.
3. Put the ham in a large turkey roasting oven sack and put in a backing tray.
4. Spill cola over the ham. Eliminate the maximum amount of air possible and stamp the bag.
5. Jab some holes in the bag to allow the steam escape and cook between 4 to 5 hours. Remove excess juice and slice.

Cornish Hens with Honey and Poppy Seeds

Honey is something sweet and very nutritious. Did you know that it's the only food without expiration date? And turkey... we have so many adjectives to describe some delicious and soft turkey that we can't simply tag it with one. If you're a lover of both foods, then this recipe will amaze you.

Yields: Makes 4 servings.

Ingredients
2 Rock Cornish hens
1/2 teaspoon black pepper, ground
1/3 cup honey
1/2 teaspoon salt
1 tablespoon poppy seeds
1 1/2 teaspoon mustard, ground
3/4 ginger, ginger

Method of preparation
1. Heat the oven to 350 degrees Fahrenheit.
2. Sprinkle non-stick spray over the rack of shallow roasting tray non-stick.
3. Cut each hen in half; place skin side down each half in the roasting tray.
4. Drizzle with pepper and salt.
5. Mix the honey, mustard, ginger and honey. Stir well.
6. Roast uncovered for 1 hour. Turn just one time and repeat.

Meatloaf for Thanksgiving

This is a traditional and delicious recipe for Thanksgiving. Make sure to prepare it with some additional turkey to complete your dinner.

Yields: Makes 1 9-by-5 inch meat loaf.

Ingredients
2 large eggs
2 1/2 pounds turkey, ground
1/3 cup milk
1 1/2 cups stuffing, chicken flavor

Method of preparation
1. Heat the oven to 350 degrees Fahrenheit.
2. In a large mixing bowl, incorporate stuffing, eggs, milk, turkey, and mix well.
3. The mixture texture will be lumpy.
4. In a 9 by 5-inch bread pan, spread the mixture.
5. Bake for 1 hour or until the temperature measured in the center of the loaf is 165 degrees Fahrenheit.

Navy Style Roasted Turkey

The meat is so tender that will delight your tongue and palate; the taste is so amazing that will take you to heaven and back; the preparation is easier than your think that will save you some serious time.

Yields: Makes 15 servings.

Ingredients
18 whole turkey, thawed
1 pound baby carrots
1 1/4 cups cold butter, quartered
2 large onions, coarsely minced
3 stalks celery, coarsely minced
1 complete head garlic, cut in half crosswise
3 tablespoons sage, fresh and minced
3 tablespoons thyme, fresh and minced
2 bay leaves
750 milliliter chilled Chardonnay wine
Salt
Black pepper, ground

Method of preparation
1. Heat the oven to 300 degrees Fahrenheit. Put a turkey roasting rack in a roasting tray.
2. Remove the giblet and neck package from the interior of the turkey, if any, and wash the turkey in depth, inside and out.
3. Pat dry the turkey.

4. Transfer the turkey to the roasting rack.
5. Loosen the turkey skin.
6. Put the butter dices and distribute equally underneath the whole breast.
7. To secure the skin, insert 4 or 5 wooden toothpicks through the skin into the meat.
8. Mix the two garlic head halves, carrots, celery, onions, thyme, sage, bay leaves, black pepper, and salt in a bowl.
9. Fill the cavity of the turkey with as many vegetables and seasoning as possible.
10. Lift the turkey vertically so the opening of the cavity is upmost, then empty the whole bottle of Chardonnay into the bird; that way the wine flows into the tray.
11. Lay back down the turkey onto the rack and, if desired, truss.
12. Cover turkey with aluminum foil.
13. Roast in the oven for 7 hours or until the bone is no longer pink, and the juices run clear.
14. Take out the turkey of the oven, remove the aluminum foil, and roast for 25-30 minutes until the skins turns crisp and brown.
15. In the thickest part of the thigh, insert and instant-read thermometer and this should measure 180 degrees Fahrenheit.
16. Take out of the oven and let cool for 10 minutes before serving.

Orange Duck

Couldn't find a turkey anywhere? Well, the great news for you is that duck is a great alternative for turkey, and this one will definitely show you know why you should consider preparing some duck for dinner instead of turkey from now on.

Yields: Makes 4 servings

Ingredients
4 duck breast halves
12 ounces orange marmalade
1 small yellow onion, sliced
1 small orange, sliced
2 cloves garlic, chopped

Method of preparation
1. Heat the oven to 475 degrees Fahrenheit.
2. Grease a glass-baking pan of 1 1/2 quart with lid.
3. In the bottom of the prepared baking pan, spread 1/4 cup of orange marmalade.
4. Put the duck breasts in the dish right on the marmalade.
5. Prick the breasts entirely using a fork.
6. Spread 1 tablespoons layer of marmalade on each breast.
7. Drizzle garlic over the top of the duck meat.
8. Spread the orange slices and onion around the duck meat in the pan.

9. Cover the pan with the lid, and bake in the oven for 15 minutes, or until the interior of the duck breasts measure 100 degrees Fahrenheit.
10. Remove the lid and return to oven after spreading over each breast 1 tablespoon of orange marmalade.
11. Bake the meat until is medium or it reaches 145 degrees Fahrenheit.

Perfectly Roasted Turkey

To eat or not to eat? That's the question. You might have been thinking this over and over again throughout the year, but not today! It's thanksgiving. We guarantee that this turkey will erase that question from your head (at least for today.) But don't worry; it'll be our secret.

Yields: Makes 24 servings.

Ingredients
18 pounds whole turkey
1/2 unsalted butter
Salt
Ground pepper
8 cups stuffing, prepared
1 1/2 quarts turkey broth

Method of preparation
1. Heat the oven to 325 degrees Fahrenheit.
2. In the lowest location of the oven, place the rack.
3. Remove the giblets and neck of the turkey, wash it, and pat dry using towels.
4. Breast side pointing up; place the turkey on a rack in the roasting tray.
5. Fill the cavity of the body with filler.
6. Apply the butter all over the skin of the turkey, and add salt and pepper to season.
7. Wrap the turkey with aluminum foil.

8. Add 2 cups of turkey broth into the bottom of the roasting tray.
9. Sprinkle the juices on the bottom of the tray periodically (30 minutes) over the turkey.

10. Add broth to moisten the juices once they have evaporated. About 1 to 2 cups at a time.
11. After 2 hours, remove the aluminum foil.
12. Roast until the thermometer in thigh of the turkey measures 180 degrees Fahrenheit, up to 4 hours.
13. Put the turkey on a large serving tray, and let cool for 20-30 minutes before serving.

Roasted Apple Cider Turkey

Want to give your turkey a different flavor, but at the same time something unforgettable? You'll find that sometimes you just need to try news things to impress your family or guests. Don't worry, we already try this recipe, it's GREAT.

Yields: Makes 15 servings

Ingredients
16 pounds whole turkey, giblets and neck removes
1 1/2 gallon water
1 cup sugar, white
1/4 cup olive oil, extra virgin
1/4 teaspoon dried thyme
1/4 teaspoon poultry seasoning
1 gallon apple cider
1 1/2 cups kosher salt

Method of preparation
1. Wash the inside and out of the turkey with water; pat dry.
2. In a large saucepan, mix sugar, kosher salt, apple cider, and water. Stir to disintegrate sugar and salt.
3. Submerge in the brine the turkey; cover the recipient, and transfer to the refrigerator. 8 hours as minimum, and overnight as maximum.
4. Preheat the oven to 325 degrees Fahrenheit.

5. Take the turkey out of the brine and eliminate the used brine.
6. Put the turkey in a roasting tray with the breast side pointing up.
7. Pat dry the turkey and cavity using paper towels.
8. Ease the skin of the turkey over the thighs and breast using your fingers.
9. In a small bowl, mix thyme poultry seasoning and olive oil.
10. Rub the oil mixture underneath the loosened skin and over thru turkey.
11. Cover the turkey completely using aluminum foil.
12. Insert a thermometer into the thickest part of thigh, don't reach the bone, and roast in the oven until it measures between 165 or 175 degrees Fahrenheit.
13. Wait 45 minutes before removing the foil to allow the skin brown.
14. Allow the turkey cool for 30 or 45 minutes before serving.

Roasted Turkey with Herbs

Ready to have some soft and delicious turkey? Who isn't? After all this what we've been waiting for! Try it with some of our savory side dishes.

Yields: Makes 12 pounds of Turkey.

Ingredients
12 pound whole turkey
1 teaspoon salvia, ground
1 teaspoon salt
1/2 teaspoon black pepper, ground
2 cups water
2 teaspoons dried basil
3/4 cup olive oil
2 tablespoons garlic, ground

Method of preparation
1. Heat oven to 325 degrees Fahrenheit.
2. Clean the Turkey; that is, discard organs and giblets.
3. Place the turkey in a roasting covered casserole.
4. Combine ground garlic, pepper, salt, ground sage, dried basil and olive oil in a small mixing bowl.
5. Brush the mixture on the uncooked turkey using a basting brush.
6. Aggregate water in the bottom of the roasting casserole, and cover with the lid.

7. Bake until the thermometer reads a temperature of 180 degrees Fahrenheit in the thickest part of the thigh. Between 3 and 3 1/2 hours.
8. Take the turkey out of the oven and allow cooling for about 30 minutes before serving.

Simple Turkey in a Bag

Don't let the title deceive you. I mean, it's a simple turkey in a bag recipe. But this one is different from the others. Why? Because it's perfectly cooked tender and its taste is unbelievable!

Yields: Makes 12 servings.

Ingredients
12 pounds whole turkey
Salt
Ground pepper
2 tablespoons all-purpose flour
2 large onions, diced
5 stalks celery

Method of preparation
1. Heat oven to 350 degrees Fahrenheit
2. Remove giblets and wash turkey. Add pepper and salt to taste.
3. Drizzle with flour the bottom of a turkey roasting oven bag.
4. Transfer the turkey along with the onions and celery to the bag.
5. Stamp bag and prick the bad using a fork.
6. Cook between 3 to 3 1/2 hours, or until the internal temperature measured with a thermometer in the thigh reads 180 degrees Fahrenheit.

Smoked Turkey

Try this 5-stars smoked turkey that will give your dinner a heavenly touch that will delight your guests. Don't be surprised if they ask you for the recipe at the end of the dinner!

Yields: Makes 1 turkey.

Ingredients
10 pounds whole turkey, giblets and neck removed
1 apple, diced
1 onion, diced
1 tablespoon salt
1 tablespoon pepper, ground
1 tablespoon ground garlic
2 cans soda cola-flavored, carbonated
1/2 cup butter
2 tablespoons seasoned salt
4 cloves garlic, crushed

Method of preparation
1. Heat smoker to 225 to 250 degrees Fahrenheit
2. Wash turkey with cold water, and pat dry.
3. Rub the garlic over the skin of the bird, and drizzle with seasoned salt.
4. Transfer turkey to a roasting tray.
5. Put cola, ground pepper, salt, butter, apple, onion and ground garlic within the cavity of the turkey.
6. Cover the roasting tray with aluminum foil.

7. Smoke for 10 hours at 225 to 250 degrees Fahrenheit or when the meat thermometer inside of the thigh reads 180 degrees Fahrenheit.
8. Drizzle every 1 or 2 hours the bird with the juices located at the bottom of the roasting tray.

Stuffed Pumpkin

Sometimes it's easier to be happy than you think. Pumpkins are so sweet and are it's always been some classic on every table for Thanksgiving. You will find out that some soft and delectable pumpkin will make you smile more than you every thought!

Yields: Makes 8 servings.

Ingredients
1 medium-sized sugar pumpkin
1 cup wild rice
2 teaspoons salt
1/2 tablespoon mustard
2 tablespoons bacon fat
1 pound venison, ground
1 onion, finely chopped
2 large eggs, beaten
1/2 teaspoon black pepper, ground
1 teaspoon sage, dried

Method of preparation
1. Bring 4 cups of water to a boil in a pot.
2. Incorporate wild rice and stir.
3. Reduce heat, place the lid and simmer for 1 hour, until soft.
4. Heat the oven to 350 degrees Fahrenheit.
5. Scoop out the pulp and seeds of the pumpkin after removing the top.

6. Poke the interior of the pumpkin using a fork, and rub turkey with 1 teaspoon salt and mustard.
7. In a large frying pan, heat the bacon fat over medium-high heat.
8. Incorporate the onion, ground venison, and stir.
9. Cook gently and keep stirring until equally brown.
10. Remove from heat.
11. Mix in the eggs, sage, pepper, wild rice and reaming salt.
12. Fill the pumpkin with the venison stuffing.
13. Place the pumpkin in a flat baking tray and cover with 1/2 inch water.
14. Bake the pumpkin for 1 1/2 hours, or until the pumpkin is soft and tender.
15. To avoid it from sticking, add more water to the tray.

Stuffed Pumpkin II

Ever tasted something so delicious that your wished it'd have never ended? Well, this delicious pumpkin filled with delicious vegetables, cheese and butter will definitely make you forget about the turkey (well, perhaps I exaggerated. There's nothing better than having some delicious turkey for dinner.)

Yields: Makes 12 servings.

Ingredients
1/2 cup almonds, sliced
1 teaspoon butter
1 onion, chopped
2 large eggs, slightly beaten
1/2 cup mayonnaise
10.75 ounces can condensed cream of mushroom soup
14 ounces frozen and drained broccoli, thawed and chopped
Salt
Pepper
1/3 cups grated Cheddar cheese
16 ounces package herb seasoned stuffing mix
1/2 cup melted butter
1 large pumpkin with the top removed, seeded

Method of preparation
1. Heat the oven to 350 degrees Fahrenheit

2. Put the almonds over medium heat in a frying pan, and stirring continuously, cook for 5 minutes until delicately toasted.
3. Melt over medium heat the tablespoon of butter in a frying pan, and fry the onion until fork tender.
4. Mix the eggs, cream of mushroom soup, broccoli and onion in a bowl.
5. Add salt and pepper to season.
6. Scoop into the pumpkin, 1/3 of the mixture.
7. Layer with 1/3 filler plus 1/3 cup Cheddar cheese.
8. Sprinkle with 1/3 melted butter.
9. Drizzle with 1/3 toasted almonds.
10. Repeat the layers one time.
11. Transfer pumpkin to a baking sheet.
12. Bake for 1 hour the pumpkin or until the stuffing is hot and bubbly.
13. For the stuffing to begin to brown, cover with aluminum the top of the pumpkin.

Super Turkey

Want to be amazed your tongue with some tasty turkey filled with some delightful stuffing that will make you think that it should be a crime to enjoy something so much! Yummy!

Yields: Makes 12 servings.

Ingredients
12 pounds whole turkey, giblets and neck removed
1/2 cup butter, diced
1 cup celery, chopped
1 1/2 cup toasted bread, diced
1/4 cup onion, chopped
1 tablespoon garlic, ground
Salt
Pepper
2 apples, cored and cut in half
2 cups apple juice

Method of preparation
1. Heat the oven to 350 degrees Fahrenheit.
2. Carefully ease the skin on the breast of the turkey by sliding the hand between the skin and bird.
3. Insert dices of butter between of the breast and skin.
4. In a medium mix bowl, throw bread dices, celery, and onion. Add ground garlic, pepper and salt to season.

5. Stuff the mixture into the cavity of the turkey along with the pieces of the apple.
6. Place the turkey into a roasting oven bag, and spill the apple juice inside of the turkey and outside.
7. Stamp the bag and place the turkey into a large roasting tray with the breast pointing up.
8. Bake until the temperature in the meatiest part of the thigh read 180 Fahrenheit degrees; that is, up to 3 1/2 hours.
9. Open the bag and transfer the turkey to a serving tray.
10. Let cool for 20 minutes before serving.

Thanksgiving Turkey Prepared in Slow Cooker

Want to prepare your turkey but have other things to do? Try this recipe! You won't have to worry about your turkey, and you'll be able to spend your day with your family.

Yields: Makes 12 servings.

Ingredients
5 bacon strips
5 1/2 pound bone-in with skin removed turkey
1/2 teaspoon garlic pepper
1 teaspoon dried sage
2 tablespoons all-purpose flour
1 can turkey gravy
1 tablespoon sauce Worcestershire

Method of preparation
1. In a frying pan over medium-high heat, place the bacon and cook it until smoothly brown. Drain and mince.
2. Sprinkle the slow cooker with cooking spray.
3. Transfer the turkey to the slow cooker.
4. Add garlic pepper to season.
5. Mix the gravy, Worcestershire sauce, sage, and bacon in a mixing bowl.
6. Spill over the turkey in the slow cooker.

7. Place the lid on the slow cooker and cook the turkey for 8 hours on low mode.

Turkey Legs prepared in Slow Cooker

This is an alternative and effective recipe if you want to have hot food for your thanksgiving dinner, and at the same time you want to spend time buying ingredients for your Thanksgiving dinner.

Yields: Makes 6 servings.

Ingredients
6 turkey legs
6 12 by 16-inch squares of aluminum foil
3 teaspoon divided of poultry seasoning
Salt
Ground pepper

Method of preparation
1. Rinse the turkey legs, and shake to remove excess humidity.
2. Drizzle about 1/2 teaspoon of poultry, pepper and salt over each turkey leg.
3. Pack tightly each leg with aluminum foil.
4. Transfer the packed legs into a slow cooker making sure they don't content liquids or other ingredients.
5. Set slow cooker to low mode, and cook for up to 7-8 hours until the meat is fork tender.

Side Dishes

Bananas and Honey with Whipped Sweet Potatoes

Even though this is a very unusual dish for Thanksgiving, it's a great option to create a festival of flavors on your table. This is also a great option for people who want to have some healthy food.

Yields: Makes 10-12 servings.

Ingredients
5 medium sweet potatoes (washed.)
4 bananas
2 bars butter (unsalted.)
1/4 cup honey
1/2 cup all-purpose flour
1/4 cup dark sugar
1 1/2 cups pecans (chopped.)

Method of preparation
1. Heat the oven 375 degrees Fahrenheit.
2. Prick the potatoes all over using a fork.
3. Transfer them to a broiler pan and roast for 30 minutes.
4. Put the bananas into the pan and roast for another 10-15 minutes until the potatoes and bananas are just fork tender.

5. Take the out the pan of the oven but don't turn it off.
6. Let the potatoes chill until are they are cool enough to handle.
7. In a large mixing bowl, peel the potatoes to remove the skin.
8. Add the bananas peeled, 1 bar of butter, and honey to the bowl.
9. Add salt to season and whip actively using a wooden spoon until all the ingredients are completely combined and the mixture is creamy.
10. Transfer the mix to an ovenproof serving dish and smooth the top.
11. Use your finger to rub the butter equally along with the brown sugar, flour, and pecans in a separate mixing dish until the mixture has the consistency of coarse crumbs.
12. Sprinkle with crumb mixture on over sweet potatoes and bring back to the oven.
13. Bake for 20 minutes making sure to obtain golden crumbs.
14. Serve hot.

Butternut Squash Macaroni and Cheese

Who said Macaroni and Cheese? Here you have the amazing fixings of macaroni and cheese pasta with all the flavor and texture of delicious butternut squash. You might think that homemade pasta could be a difficult duty, but I assure you that this meal is worth the extra time in the kitchen!

Yields: Makes 5 servings.

Ingredients
1 pound lined macaroni; you can either use tubatini or mini penne rigate.
Salt
1 tablespoon extra-virgin olive oil
2 tablespoons unsalted butter
2 tablespoons thyme leaves, fresh and chopped.
1/2 onion, medium size
Sprigs (for decoration purposes.)
3 tablespoons flour, all-purpose
2 cups chicken broth
10 ounces of frozen butternut squash, thawed
1 cup of cream
2 cups sharp Cheddar cheese, shredded
1/2 cup of Parmigiano-Reggiano cheese, shredded
1/4 teaspoon nutmeg, ground
Pepper, ground

Method of preparation

1. Using a pot, bring water to boil.
2. Add salt to the water and then aggregate the pasta. Cook the pasta to "al dente."
3. While the pasta is cooking, over medium heat, heat a medium heavy bottomed saucepan.
4. Aggregate the extra-virgin olive oil and butter.
5. Once the butter melts into the saucepan, aggregate thyme.
6. Scrape the onion using a Microplane, and add it directly into the saucepan.
7. For 1 or 2 minutes, cook the butter in butter and oil.
8. Aggregate the flour, and cook for 1 or 2 more minutes.
9. Whisk all the ingredients in the saucepan.
10. Add the butternut squash and cook until warm and soft.
11. Add the cream and mix. Bring sauce to a bubble.
12. Add all the cheeses and mix. Aggregate the salt, nutmeg, and pepper to finish seasoning.
13. Adjust seasoning by tasting the sauce.
14. Remove the excess water of the pasta well, add the sauce and stir well.
15. Serve it with the thyme leaves on top.

Corn and Pumpkin Bread

Looking for something to eat your turkey with? Here we have this delightful bread with two key ingredients that you can forget this thanksgiving: corn and pumpkin! Yummy! You dinner will never be same after you put your teeth on one of these.

Yields: Makes 7 3/4 dozen.

Ingredients
13 eggs
2 1/2 pounds pumpkin
5 3/4 cups yellow or white cornmeal
2 1/2 tablespoons baking soda
5 3/4 cups flour
1 1/2 tablespoon salt
3 cups sugar
2 1/2 baking powder
3/4 teaspoon cinnamon
Nutmeg
1 pound butter, unsalted and melted

Method of preparation
1. Preheat the oven to 350 degrees Fahrenheit.
2. Take 7 cupcakes pans and grease them.
3. In another bowl, mix the buttermilk, pumpkin, eggs and sugar until completely mix. Put aside.
4. Blending in depth, add the pumpkin mix to the dry ingredients.

5. Incorporate melted butter and stir.
6. Aggregate 2 ounces of mixture in each muffin cup of the prepared tin.
7. Bake for 15-20 minutes until a toothpick comes out clean.

Cranberry Sauce with Honey

This recipe could be confused with a dessert. Well, we can be more than happy that it's considered a side dish because we get to have some dessert before time. But, hey, keep it under the table. This recipe will definitely add a sweet touch to your dinner.

Yields: Makes 6 to 8 servings.

Ingredients
1/4 cup squeezed orange juice, fresh
1 cup honey
1/4 cup 100% cranberry juice
4 cups fresh cranberries

Method of preparation
1. Wash the cranberries and dismiss any spoiled or tender ones.
2. In a 2-quart pan, combine the cranberry juice, orange juice and honey over medium-high heat.
3. Bring to a boil and simmer for 5 minutes.
4. Incorporate the cranberries and cook for another 15 minutes, mixing once in a while, until the cranberries start to pop and the mixture is soupy.
5. Take away from the heat.
6. Chill for 5 minutes.
7. Into a 3-cup mold, spoon the sauce cautiously and put in the refrigerator for at least 7 hours and up to 8 hours.

8. Take out of the refrigerator, turn the mold over and slide the sauce out.

Green Bean and Mushroom Casserole

Tired of your casserole recipe? Discover this succulent and easy to cook casserole. Everyone will expect this classic dish on your thanksgiving dinner. After all, who doesn't love the classic casserole with green beans and fresh vegetables? Who could blame them?

Yields: Makes 6-8 servings.

6 cups green beans
3 tablespoons butter
1 loaf crunchy bread, Italian
3 tablespoons fresh chives, chopped
1 tablespoon rosemary leaves, chopped
4 tablespoons Parmesan cheese, shredded
Kosher salt
Pepper, ground
3 tablespoons thyme leaves, fresh and chopped
4 cups mixed mushrooms, sliced
2 shallots, sliced
1 cup heavy cream
5 1/4 tablespoons extra virgin olive oil

Method of preparation
1. Add water to a large saucepan and bring up to boil.
2. Aggregate a dash of salt and the green beans.
3. After cooking the beans for 5 minutes, drain the excess water and put them aside. (The beans should

be still crisp. But don't worry; they will cook more in the oven.)
4. Butter a large baking pan enough to sustain the beans with 1 tablespoon butter and put aside.
5. Pre heat the oven to 375 degrees Fahrenheit.
6. Rip the bread into 2-inch pieces, put the 2 parts into a bowl, and incorporate 1 tablespoon chives, 1 tablespoon rosemary, 1 tablespoon thyme, 3 tablespoons extra virgin olive oil, and 2 tablespoons of Parmesan cheese.
7. Bake for around 10 minutes, just until the bread starts to turn golden.
8. Take out of the oven and put aside.
9. Over medium heat, melt the rest of the butter and olive oil in a large frying pan.
10. Incorporate shallots and mixed mushrooms.
11. Add pepper and salt to season and cook for about 10 minutes, just until the mix mushrooms have released their liquid.
12. Aggregate the heavy cream, the remaining chives, the remaining thyme, and cook for 5 minutes.
13. Incorporate the green beans and mix well.
14. Transfer the green beans mixtures into the already prepared baking pan, put the croutons on top, and spray the Parmesan cheese on.
15. Bake for 20-25 minutes until everything is hot bubbling.

Mashed Potatoes gently baked and prepared with Parmesan Cheese and Bread Crumbs

Today's side dish is some delicious and creamy mashed potatoes with Parmesan cheese and breadcrumbs. What makes this dish so succulent? Perhaps it's its consistency? Perhaps its flavor? We have no idea! But we are sure that Mashed potatoes are ideal to accompany with some delightful turkey.

Yields: Makes 6-8 servings.

Ingredients
1 tablespoon butter, salty
8 cups (4 pounds) russet potatoes, cut into 1-inch bulks and peeled
1 cup milk, whole
1 bar melted butter. (1/2 cup.)
1 1/2 cups mozzarella cheese, shredded
1 cup grated Parmesan Cheese, shredded
Salt
Black pepper, ground
2 tablespoons breadcrumbs, dry

Method of preparation
1. Preheat the oven to 400-Farehneit degrees.
2. Grab a 13x9x2-inch baking tray. Put aside.
3. In a casserole, add some water and salt.

4. Transfer the potatoes to the casserole. Cook them until they are fork tender.
5. Drain excess water and put the potatoes back into the casserole and mash them.
6. Melt the butter in the microwave using a small bowl.
7. Add in the milk and melted butter to the potatoes. Stir well until fully incorporated.
8. Add in 3/4 cup of mozzarella and Parmesan cheese.
9. Mix well.
10. Pass the potatoes to the prepared baking tray.
11. Take a small bowl; add the 1/4-cup of Parmesan cheese along with the breadcrumbs.
12. Stir well.
13. Scatter the breadcrumb mix on top of the mashed potatoes.
14. Cover and cool.
15. Transfer to oven, and keeping uncovered, bake for about 20 minutes or until the surface presents a golden brown.

Mashed Potatoes prepared with Sour Cream and Chive

Getting ready for Thanksgiving? Looking for something easy and delicious to prepare? Today I bring you this appetizing dish. What could be better than your family together, some turkey, and mashed potatoes with sour cream? Super succulent!

Yields: Makes 6 servings.

Ingredients
2 pounds Yukon gold potatoes, cut into 1-inch blocks and peeled.
8 tablespoons of melted butter, unsalted
1/2-cup sour cream
1/2 half-and-half
1/4-cup chives, minced
1/10-cup chives for decoration
Kosher salt
Black pepper, ground

Method of preparation
1. In a large casserole, add the potatoes, and add enough cold water to cover them by at least 1 inch.
2. Bring to a boil, and then decrease the heat to low.
3. Cook the potatoes until fork tender. Up to 20 minutes.

4. Over low heat combine butter and half-and-half in a small saucepan. Cook until hot, but not simmering.
5. Drain the potatoes. Make sure to get rid of excess water.
6. Clean the casserole until completely dry.
7. Pass the potatoes through a food mill back into the casserole.
8. Using a hand mixer, give the mashed potatoes a quick stir to add some air and guarantee a creamy texture. Do not stir too much; otherwise, the potatoes will become too gummy.
9. Fold in the melted butter and half-half mixture using a malleable spatula until completely incorporated.
10. Add in 1/4-cup chives and the sour cream. Use the salt and pepper to season.
11. Move to the serving bowl and decorate using the remaining chopped chives.

Mashed Potatoes with Truffles and Cheese

Seafood lover? Cheese lover? Mashed potatoes lover? Great news! Here you have this delicious and tasty recipe prepared with these three delightful ingredients. This Thanksgiving make sure to astonish your guests with some mashed potatoes, cheese and truffles. Yummy!

Yields: Makes 4-6 servings.

Ingredients
2 pounds washed large potatoes.
Kosher salt
1 1/2 cups Sottocenere al Tartufo cheese, shredded
1 cup cream
8 tablespoons butter, unsalted
Black pepper, ground

Method of preparation
1. In a large casserole, put the potatoes.
2. Add cold water until it's covered by 1 inch.
3. Aggregate 2 tablespoons of kosher salt.
4. Over high heat, bring to a boil. Make sure it's uncovered.
5. Reduce to medium or high heat and cook gently until the potatoes are tender. This should take 45 minutes.
6. Drain the water of the potatoes.

7. Cut the potatoes in quarters and peel the potatoes. (Don't peel them if you're using a food mill.)
8. Pass the potatoes through a ricer and bring them back to the pan.
9. When the potatoes are almost ready, over medium heat, warm the cream in a small casserole and cook gently. Up to 5 minutes.
10. Incorporate the cheese and stir until completely melted.
11. Put aside.
12. Take the hot cheese and cream, and pour it over the potatoes.
13. Reduce to low heat, and add small pieces of butter, fragment by fragment, until completely incorporated.
14. Add pepper and salt to season.
15. Serve hot.

Mushroom and Broccoli with Cheese

Cheese is very delicious, and contrary to what you might think, it doesn't contain too many calories. But if you feel guilty, you can try it with some delicious broccoli. Broccoli has always been known as an excellent vegetable with excellent properties for your body. Something delicious and healthy! Great!

Yields: Makes 6-8 servings.

Ingredients
4 tablespoons butter
1 cup baby bella mushrooms, sliced
2 tablespoon all-purpose flour
1/4 cup chopped onions
2 cloves garlic, gently minced
1/2 teaspoon garlic, powder
1/3 teaspoon pepper, cayenne
1 1/2 cups heavy cream
1/2 cup chicken broth
1 1/4 cup broccoli, chopped
2 cups Cheddar-Monterey cheese, shredded and blended
3 cups cooked rice
Salt
Pepper, ground

Method of preparation
1. Preheat the oven to 425 degrees Fahrenheit.

2. Butter casserole pot.
3. In a large saucepan over medium heat, melt 3 tablespoons of butter and flour to make a quick roux. The roux should have the color of peanut butter.
4. Aggregate these ingredients: onion, garlic powder, cayenne pepper, heavy cream, chicken broth and garlic.
5. Incorporate broccoli, the cooked rice and 1 cup of cheese.
6. Pass the mix to the already buttered pot and sprinkle the remaining shredded Cheddar.
7. Bake for 20 minutes until cheese looks golden and melted.

Quick Rolls

These rolls will become your best ally when having some turkey with stuffing. It doesn't matter if it's the first time you cook, they will still look great, and will taste like heaven.

Yields: Makes 24 dinner rolls.

Ingredients
1/4 ounce active dry yeast
1 3/4 warm water
3 teaspoons salt
2 large eggs, beaten
1/2 cup honey
5-6 cups flours

Method of preparation
1. Heat the oven to 400 degrees Fahrenheit.
2. With the bowl of a stand mixer fitted with the palette attachment, combine the instant yeast, and warm water.
3. Whip for 5 minutes until it becomes the bubbly.
4. Incorporate the honey and whip.
5. Reduce to low speed and incorporate 2 teaspoons salt, 2 eggs and ½ cup of melted butter.
6. Gently add cup-by-cup the flour until completely incorporated and the paste pulls away from the sides of the mixing dish.
7. Aggregate more flour if it's too viscous.

8. Separate the paste into 24 portions.
9. Shape into desired form the bulks.
10. Transfer the bulks to a frying pan or to a baking sheet.
11. Put aside for about 20 minutes and allow them to rise, or until they are twice its size.
12. Brush the rolls with melted butter.
13. Take the rolls to the oven a bake for 25 minutes until top has a golden brown aspect.
14. Take out of the oven and brush more melted butter on top.
15. Sprinkle with a pinch of salt.

Roasted Cauliflower with Butter and Garlic

Don't be deceived by the name of this recipe. Even though it's a very simple recipe, it's full of flavors, color, and texture to enrich and melt your guests' mouth.

Yields: Makes 4 servings.

Ingredients
3 tablespoons vegetable oil
4 cloves garlic, finely chopped
1/4 cup Japanese bread crumbs
Kosher salt
Black pepper, ground
1 tablespoon butter, cut into 4 pieces
1 head cauliflower, cut into florets
1 tablespoon cumin seeds, coarsely ground

Ingredients
1. Heat the oven to 425 degrees Fahrenheit.
2. Throw the oil, cauliflower, garlic and cumin in a bowl, and toss to incorporate.
3. Use black pepper and salt to adjust the seasoning
4. Put the mixture to a baking pan and sprinkle the butter over the mixture.
5. Drizzle the Japanese breadcrumbs over the cauliflower.

6. Put the baking dish in the oven and roast for 20-30 minutes, or until the cauliflower is tender and golden brown.

Roasted Sweet Potatoes with Honey and Cinnamon

Looking for some marshmallows and honey? You'd better forget about that! Try this dish instead. It's more tasteful and it has less calories.

Yields: Makes 4 servings.

Ingredients
4 sweet potatoes
1/2 cup olive oil, extra virgin
1/4 cup honey
2 teaspoons cinnamon, ground
Salt
Black pepper

Method of preparation
1. Heat the oven to 375 degrees Fahrenheit.
2. Peel and cut the potatoes into 1-inch cubes and put on a roasting pan.
3. Sprinkle the olive oil, cinnamon, salt, honey and pepper over the potatoes.
4. Roast in the oven for about 25-30 minutes or until fork tender.
5. Take the potatoes out of the oven and put them into a serving tray.
6. Sprinkle with more olive oil.

Soft Sweet Corn Bread

Corn has always been and will always be a traditional side dish for Thanksgiving, and it's even tastier as bread. It's soft in the inside, crunchy on the outside; it's delightful, and warm. Make sure to bake some of this bread to transform your turkey into a new great experience.

Yields: Makes 6-8 servings.

Ingredients
1/2 onion, cut into 1-inch cubes
1/2 teaspoon thyme leaves, fresh
1 ounce unsalted butter
15 ounces (1 can) cream-style sweet corn
2 large eggs
1 cup heavy cream
1 teaspoon baking powder
1/2 cup stone whole grain cornmeal, ground
1/2 cup Parmesan cheese, shredded
Kosher salt
2 cup French bread, cut into 1-inch cubes
Black pepper, ground

Method of preparation
1. Pre heat the oven to 350 degrees Fahrenheit.
2. In an oven safe pan, sweat the onions with herbs and butter until translucent.

3. In a large mixing bowl, incorporate and mix cream, baking powder, corn, eggs, cornmeal, salt, pepper, and Parmesan cheese.
4. Add the cubes of bread and stir to combine.
5. Sprinkle the paste right over the onion mixture.
6. Bake for 50 minutes, or until set.
7. Chill lightly before serving.

Tricolor Mashed Potatoes

Looking for something colorful? Well, these mashed potatoes don't look simply colorful; they're delicious too! Mashed potatoes have always been a delicious dish to eat on Thanksgiving, and it's preparation is very simple.

Yields: Makes 4 servings.

Ingredients
4 cups quartered red new potatoes
2 cloves smashed garlic
1/4 pound Gorgonzola cheese at room temperature
1/4 cup heavy creams at room temperature
Salt
Ground pepper
1 tablespoon unsalted butter

Method of preparation
1. In a medium saucepan, add the new red potatoes and garlic.
2. Add water until the potatoes and garlic are covered by 1-inch
3. Add salt to season and bring water to boil.
4. Reduce to a simmer and cook the potatoes until fork tender. Up to 15 minutes.
5. In a skillet add bacon and fry until crisp.
6. Put the bacon aside on paper towel and allow the bacon to drain the fat.

7. Chop well and reserve.
8. Remove the excess water of the potatoes and garlic back into the saucepan.
9. Incorporate butter, heavy cream and chopped bacon.
10. Mash the ingredients roughly, and add more cream if needed.
11. Add pepper and salt to season.

Desserts
Apple Cider Apple Pie

This delicious combination of cream pie, apple cider and apple pie will definitely amaze your palate. You won't even give a little slice to your guests! This stunning marriage of flavors has to be a MUST on this thanksgiving. Its crust, its flavor, and its texture are something that you cannot simply forget. This dessert will astonish your guests.

Yields: 8 servings.

Ingredients
To make the crust
1 cup flour (all-purpose)
1 tablespoon cornflour
1 tablespoon sugar
1 teaspoon salt
1 bar butter (unsalted), divided 1/2-inch dice
3 tablespoons milk (cold)
1 teaspoon apple cider vinegar

To make stuffing and topping
1 cup granulated sugar
1/2 cup cream (sour)
4 large eggs
1/4 teaspoon salt
1 cup heavy cream

2 cups apple cider
1/2 teaspoon cinnamon

Method of preparation
1. Combine the flour, corn flour, sugar, butter and salt; and take it to a food processor.
2. Keep pressing for 1-second intervals bursts until the mix simulates coarse meal.
3. Incorporate the milk and vinegar.
4. Sprinkle it on top.
5. Keep pressing 1-second bursts until the dough joins together.
6. Take the dough onto a work surface.
7. Unite any crumbs and par into a disk.
8. Cover it with plastic wrap and refrigerate until cool. Up to 30 minutes.
9. Roll out the dough to form an 11-inch round on a floured work surface and form a scarce 1/4-inch thick.
10. Put it into a 9-inch pie plate. (Ceramic/glass. It doesn't matter.)
11. Cut the overhanging dough to 1-inch and fold it around the border of the crust.
12. Curl decoratively and cool the crust until firm. Up to 15 minutes.
13. Heat up the oven to 425 degrees Fahrenheit. Row the crust with parchment paper and load it with pie weight or dried beans.
14. Take it to the oven and put it in the third row of the oven for 15 minutes, or until the crust is barely set.

15. Take away the parchment and ceramic/metal pie weights.
16. Cover the border of the crust with fringes of foil and bake for about 15 more minutes.
17. Make sure the crust is not brown, just set, and press the bottom of the crust softly to depress it as it puffs.
18. Let chill.
19. Decrease the oven temperature to 350 degrees Fahrenheit.
20. Boil the cider until it's decreased to 1/2, using a medium saucepan. This should take 10 minutes.
21. Take the pie to the third row of the oven and bake it for 35-40 minutes, until the custard is ensemble around the border but the middle is somewhat jiggly.
22. Chill at room temperature.
23. Using an electric mixer, mix the heavy cream with 1/4 cup of sugar, and the cinnamon in a medium bowl.
24. Mix until firmly whipped.
25. Add the cream on top of the pie.
26. Cut into slices and serve.

Butter and Milk Pie

This classic desert is great to freeze and keep on hand for this Thanksgiving. It's very easy to prepare, the ingredients are very easy to find, and it's sweet, silky and decadent.

Yields: Makes 8 servings.

Ingredients
1 Piecrust
8 tablespoons butter
1 1/2 cups sugar
2 egg yolks
1 1/2 cups buttermilk
1 tablespoon lemon juice, fresh
2 large eggs, whites
1 teaspoon lemon skin, shredded
2 grates nutmeg, fresh
3 tablespoons flour

Method of preparation
1. Heat the oven to 350 degrees Fahrenheit.
2. Whisk the butter well using an electric mixer, incorporate the sugar and continue to whisk until smooth and soft.
3. Incorporate the egg yolks and continue to whisk.
4. Add the flour the continue mixing.

5. As the mixer blends the ingredients, incorporate slowly the buttermilk along with the lemon skin and juice.
6. Mix the large white eggs well in another bowl to stiff peaks.
7. Add only 1/3 of the eggs into the buttermilk mixture and stir well; repeat the same procedure with the remaining 2/3, remembering to add 1/3 at a time.
8. Pout into the crust the filling and drizzle with nutmeg.
9. Take to the oven and bake for 40 minutes or until the surface is golden brown and the filling looks firm.
10. Let cool to room temperature.

Cocoa Cream Pie

Give yourself some special treat this Thanksgiving. I'm sure that after those longs hours looking for special recipes and cooking you will be begging for something outstanding. This dessert will be the answer to all your prayers.

Yields: Makes 6 servings.

Ingredients
1 2/3 cup water
3 tablespoons corn flour
5 tablespoons cocoa
14 ounces eagle condensed milk
3 egg yolks, whipped
2 tablespoons butter
1 teaspoon vanilla
1 (9-inch) baked pastry shell

Method of preparation
1. Mix corn flour and cocoa, and water in a mixing bowl until smooth.
2. Incorporate the condensed milk and egg yolks.
3. In a saucepan, cook mixture until thick.
4. Incorporate 2 tablespoons butter and vanilla.
5. Stirring periodically let the mixture cool lightly.
6. Pour into the baked pie shell.
7. Let the pie chill.
8. Top with whipped cream.

Lime Pie with Coconut

Dessert time is here! If you enjoyed eating that soft turkey meat, you will definitely enjoy this dessert. It's filled with love, lime and coconut that will make your tongue fall in love more and more with every bite.

Yields: Makes 8 servings

Ingredients
14 ounces condensed milk, sweetened
13.5 ounces coconut milk, unsweetened
1/3 cup lime juice, fresh or bottled
7 eggs yolks
1 easy press-in piecrust, prepared with graham crackers
2 cups heavy cream, cold
2 tablespoons sugar, confectioners
3 tablespoons sweetened shredded coconut, toasted

Method of preparation
1. Heat oven to 325 degrees Fahrenheit.
2. Mix together coconut milk, condensed milk, egg yolks, and lime juice until smooth.
3. Pout the mixture into piecrust and bake for 40 minutes until set but still lightly unsteady in the middle.
4. Let it chill for 1 1/2 or 2 hours on a wire rack.
5. Refrigerate as minimum of 3 hours, and maximum of 1 day.

6. Beat sugar and cream for 3 minutes in a large bowl using an electric mixer until hard lips form.
7. Top pie with whipped cream and drizzle with toasted coconut.

Orange and Cranberry Gelatin

Feeling guilty after eating all that meatloaf, turkey, potatoes, and green beans but don't want to skip dessert? Don't worry! Try this orange and cranberry gelatin. It'll make you forget about pie. It's something appetizing and low in calories.

Yields: Makes 6 servings.

Ingredients
1 ounce unflavored gelatin
3 cups cranberry juice, cocktail
1/2 cup orange juice, fresh
6 oranges divided into segments
3/4 cup sugar

Method of preparation
1. Drizzle gelatin over 1 cup cranberry juice in a small pot.
2. Put aside for 5 minutes to blandish.
3. Over low heat, place the gelatin for 4 or 5 minutes until completely dissolved.
4. Incorporate sugar and mix for 2 or 3 minutes softly until dissolved. Remove from heat.
5. Put the gelatin mixture in a medium bowl.
6. Incorporate and stir the remaining 2 cups of cranberry juice and orange juice.
7. Before refrigerating, skim any foam from top.

8. Refrigerate for 30 or 40 minutes until dense enough to hold a line drawn by your finger.
9. Form an arrangement of orange segments in the bottom of a Bunds pan and pour gelatin over the oranges. Take to the refrigerator for at least 2 hours or until firm.
10. To take it out of the mold, immerse the bottom of the mold shortly in hot water, put the mold upside down onto a plate, and shake rigidly to drop.

Peanut Butter and Vanilla Fudge

What's better than having some turkey on thanksgiving? Probably there isn't anything better than having some turkey, but at least there are thing that will make you forget about it like this soft, tender and extremely delicious pie. Yummy!

Ingredients
2/3 cups milk, evaporated
3/4 cup butter
16 ounces jar peanut butter, crunchy
1 teaspoon vanilla
7 1/2 jar marshmallow cream
3 cups sugar

Method of preparation
1. Grease a 9 by 3-inch frying pan.
2. Add the sugar, butter and evaporated milk in a frying pan and stir well.
3. Keep stirring frequently the mixture over medium heat.
4. Bring to a boil and keep stirring and cooking for another 4 minutes.
5. Transfer the mixture to a mixing bowl and incorporate the vanilla, peanut butter and marshmallow cream and mix completely.
6. Pour equally into the serving pan and cool in the refrigerator until firm.

Pecan Pie

Looking for delicious pecan pie desserts? Trying to find an excuse to prepare it? Thanksgiving is here! You don't need more excuses to taste these crunchy and sweet pecans, and that flaky crust just like your remember.

Yields: 12 servings.

Ingredients
<u>To make pie crust</u>
3 cups all-purpose flour
1 teaspoon salt
3/4 cup salted butter
1 egg
1 tablespoon distilled white vinegar
3/4 cup vegetable shortening

<u>To make filling</u>
1 cup granulated sugar
3 tablespoons brown sugar
1/2 teaspoon salt
1 cup corn syrup
1/3 melted salted butter
1 teaspoon vanilla
3 whole beaten eggs
1 cup chopped pecans

How to prepare

1. Churn the piecrust: Combine the flour and salt in a bowl.
2. Incorporate the vegetable shortening and salted butter.
3. Mix the butter with the flour using a dough cutter until the blend resembles small pebbles.
4. Aggregate 5 tablespoons cold water, white vinegar, and the egg.
5. Stir until just combined.
6. Divide the dough in half and cool as long as needed. (You will only use half for this recipe. The rest can be reserved for another use.)
7. The next step is making the filling: Unite the granulated sugar, brown sugar, corn syrup, salt, butter, vanilla and eggs and mix them together in a bowl.
8. Preheat the oven to 350 –Fahrenheit degrees.
9. Roll out one dough half on a moderately floured surface to fit your pie pan.
10. Shed pecans in the bottom of the unbaked pie crust.
11. Spread the syrup mix over the top.
12. Cover the top and crust smoothly with foil.
13. Bake the pie for 29 minutes.
14. Take away the foil and bake for another 20 minutes. Remember not to burn the crust or pecans.
15. The pie shouldn't be very bumpy when you take it out of the oven (though it will jiggle a little.)
16. If it jiggles a lot, cover again with foil and bake for another 20 minutes or until set. Remember: the baking time varies a lot when comes to this recipe.

Sometimes it takes 55 minutes. Sometimes it takes 75!
17. Chill for several hours or overnight. Serve in small slices.

Pumpkin and Hazelnut Pie

Hazelnuts have always been something delicious to prepare, especially when it comes to desserts. This was a flavor that we couldn't simply forget about. Now imagine it mix with some soft and sweet pumpkin… it's simply delicious.

2 cups graham crackers, crumbs
3 tablespoons sugar
3 tablespoons divided hazelnut creamer
1/2 cup melted butter
8 ounces cream cheese
3/4 cup brown sugar, light
3 large eggs
15 ounces pumpkin puree
1/2 cup heavy cream
1/4 teaspoon allspice
1/2 teaspoon salt

Method of preparation
1. Preheat oven to 350 degrees Fahrenheit.
2. Mix graham crackers, 1 tablespoon hazelnut, butter and sugar using a mixing bowl until completely combined.
3. Pour the paste into a 9 by 10-inch rounded pan, and apply pressure on bottom and up the sides. Put aside.

4. To prepare the filling, mix brown sugar, cream cheese, pumpkin puree and eggs in a large bowl and stir until fully combined.
5. Stir the 2 tablespoons of hazelnut creamer, salt, allspice into heavy cream in a small cup.
6. Transfer the heavy cream paste to the pumpkin mixture and stir well to form one paste.
7. Transfer the mixture to the crust and for 35 minutes bake or until center is firm.
8. Chill to room temperature.

Pumpkin Pudding

This is a simple pumpkin pudding recipe, which distinguishes because it's incredibly smooth, tasty, and it has the flavor of a real pumpkin pie.

Ingredients
1 3/4 cups milk, skim and cold
1/2 cup pumpkin, canned
1 ounce instant vanilla pudding mix, sugar-free
1/2 teaspoon pumpkin pie spice

Method of preparation
1. In a mixing bowl, incorporate the instant pudding and milk and stir well until the mixture looks soft.
2. Incorporate the pumpkin pie and pumpkin, mix well until soft.
3. Let chill at room temperature and serve.

Two-layer Pumpkin Pie

A delicious recipe! This exquisite and soft deserve will be the star in this thanksgiving dinner. Don't miss the opportunity to impress your guests! Everybody will talk about it!

Yields: 16 servings.

Ingredients
1 cup soft cheese cream.
1 cup milk
1 tablespoon milk
1 cup whipped cream
3/4 cup pulverized Graham cookies
2 cups pumpkin
4/5 cup instant vanilla pudding
1 teaspoon ground cinnamon
1/2 teaspoon ginger powder
1/4 ground cloves

Method of preparation
1. Mix the cream cheese, the tablespoon of milk and the sugar in a big bowl and stir well.
2. Incorporate half of the pulverized Graham cookies.
3. Spread it equally on a baking tray.
4. Stir for 2 minutes the rest of the milk, the pumpkin, the species and pudding powder using a whisk. (The mix will look thick.)
5. Diffuse this mix over the cream cheese layer.

6. Place it in the refrigerator for 4 hours or until firm.
7. At last, put the remaining layer on top before serving.

Vanilla and Carrot Soufflé

This is an easy-to-follow recipe that will delight your palate that you will prefer keeping for yourself even before dinner. This is definitely why it's worth to wait a whole year to have something as delicious as this delightful dessert.

Yields: Makes 6 servings.

Ingredients
1 pound carrots, steamed light, then smashed
1/2 cup sugar
1/2 cup butter, softened, neither melted nor warm
3 large eggs, beaten
3 tablespoons flour
1 teaspoon vanilla
1 teaspoon cinnamon, ground
1/2 teaspoon nutmeg, ground
1 teaspoon baking powder

Method of preparation
1. Heat oven to 350 degrees Fahrenheit and grease an 8 by 8-inch baking pan.
2. In a bowl, mix all ingredients using an electric mixer.
3. Transfer the mixture to the baking pan.
4. Bake until the knife comes out clean, up to 50 minutes.
5. Serve hot or cold.

Part 2

Chapter 1: Canapés and Salads

(1) Marinated Eel - Anguilla Marinata

Marinated eel is spicy and has a strong flavor. It is typically eaten as an antipasto in Italy, and eels are a specialty during the festive season. Anguilla Marinata is a dish typically eaten as an antipasto in Italy, and eels are a specialty in the capital city of Rome.

Serving Size: 4-6
Preparation Time: 10mins
Cook Time: 40mins
Total Cooking Time: 24hour 50mins
Ingredient List:

- 1 cup extra virgin olive oil
- 4 cups onions (thinly sliced)
- 6 cloves garlic (sliced)

- ½ teaspoons dried thyme
- 2 bay leaves (crumbled)
- 8 peppercorns
- 1 tablespoon salt
- 1 cup white wine vinegar
- 1 cup cold water
- 2 pounds eel (cleaned, sliced into 3" pieces)
- ¼ cup freshly squeezed lemon juice
- Flour
- 1-4 tablespoons olive oil

Methods:
1. In a heavy pan or pot, preferably 2-3 quarts, heat 1 cup of virgin olive oil.
2. Add the onions along with the garlic, thyme, bay leaves, peppercorns and salt and over medium heat, cook, while frequently stirring, for 7-8 minutes, or until the onions are translucent but not browned.
3. Pour in the vinegar along with the water, and bring to boil, reducing the heat and simmering the marinade for 20 minutes.
4. In the meantime, brush each piece of eel with fresh lemon juice and dip each piece into flour, shaking off any excess.
5. Next, heat 2 tablespoons of olive oil in a large skillet. Carefully, drop the eel into the skillet, in batches of 5-6, and cook over a medium to high heat for 4-5 minutes, adding additional olive oil if necessary.
6. Transfer the eel to a 9x12" shallow glass dish. Pour the hot marinade over the top of the eel.

7. Once the dish is at room temperature, cover the glass dish with plastic wrap and transfer it to the fridge for a minimum of 24 hours.

8. When you are ready to serve, life the eel out of the marinade and arrange on a serving platter. Moisten the pieces of eel with a drop of marinade before you are ready to serve.

(2)_Clams Casino

Clams Casino is a favorite dish served during the holidays. The recipe for Clams Casino originated in the early 20th century at Rhode Island's Casino at Narragansett Pier but soon got on to the menu in Italian-American restaurants throughout the USA.

Serving Size: 6
Preparation Time: 20mins
Cook Time: 25mins
Total Cooking Time: 45mins
Ingredient List:

- 2 tablespoons olive oil
- 2 ounces pancetta (sliced, finely chopped)
- 1 cup red bell pepper (finely diced)
- ⅓ cup shallots (chopped)
- 2 large cloves garlic (minced)
- ¼ teaspoons dried oregano
- ⅓ cup dry white wine

- 4 tablespoons Parmesan (freshly grated)
- Salt and Black Pepper
- 18 medium (2 ½") Littleneck clams (shucked, reserve bottom shells) *

Methods:

1. In a large frying pan or skillet over moderate heat, heat the oil.
2. Add the slices of pancetta and fry until golden and crispy, this will take around 3 minutes.
3. Using a slotted kitchen utensil, transfer the fried pancetta to a serving plate.
4. Add the red bell pepper along with the shallots, garlic, and oregano to the skillet and fry until the shallots are translucent and just tender, 4-5 minutes.
5. Pour in the white wine and simmer until the liquid almost completely evaporates 2-3 minutes.
6. Remove from the skillet and allow to completely cool.
7. Stir the reserved pancetta together with half of the grated Parmesan into the veggie mixture.
8. Season well to taste.
9. Preheat the main oven to 500 degrees F.
10. Line a large and heavy baking sheet with aluminum foil and arrange the Littleneck clams in their reserved shell on the sheet.
11. Spoon the veggie mixture into evenly divided mounds on top of the clams.
12. Sprinkle with the remaining Parmesan cheese and bake until the clams are cooked thoroughly, and the topping is golden and brown 8-10 minutes.

13. Arrange the clams on a serving platter and serve.
*Shucking clams isn't very easy so why not buy them pre-shucked from your seafood counter. Simply ask them to pack up the bottom shells for cooking and serving.

(3)_Seven Fishes Seafood Salad

This salad has to be the centerpiece of the feast. All seven fishes served in one huge, sharing salad along with only a few vegetables– the fish is the star of this show!

Serving Size: 10
Preparation Time: 15mins
Cook Time: 1hour 40mins
Total Cooking Time: 9hours 55mins
Ingredient List:
Salad:

- 1-pound octopus (tenderized)
- 1-pound shrimp
- 1-pound scallops
- 1-pound calamari
- 1-pound scungilli
- 1-pound baccala
- 3 pounds mussels

- For the mussels:
- ½ cup white wine

Broth:
- 3 medium cloves garlic
- 12 black peppercorns
- 3 fresh bay leaves
- 1 tablespoon fresh parsley
- 1 teaspoon fennel seeds
- 3 slices lemon peel
- ½ cup white wine
- 1 tablespoon salt

Vegetables:
- ½ cup fresh parsley (coarsely chopped)
- 1 cup celery (chopped)
- 1 cup carrots (shredded)
- 1 cup green olives stuffed with pimento

Salad dressing:
- 1 cup lemon juice (freshly squeezed)
- ¾ cup extra virgin olive oil
- 12 cloves garlic
- 1 tablespoon white wine vinegar
- Pinch oregano
- Salt (to taste)
- Red pepper flakes (to taste)

Methods:

1. First, thoroughly clean, wash and prepare as appropriate the octopus, shrimp, scallops, calamari, scungilli, baccala, and mussels.
2. To a large pot or pan, add the white wine along with the mussels. Cook the mussels until they have all completely opened and the flesh comes away from each of the shells. Remove all of the open mussels from their shells and put to one side.
3. Using a piece of clean cheesecloth, filter the mussel broth and put to one side.
4. Take a large double boiler and fill halfway with cold water.
5. Add the broth ingredients; garlic cloves, peppercorns, fresh bay leaves, parsley, fennel seeds, lemon peel, white wine, and salt to the broth.
6. Bring the water to boiling point.
7. Add, the second fish, the baccala and cook for 6-7 minutes before removing the baccala from the water and setting it to one side.
8. Add number three, the calamari, cook for 5 minutes before removing them and setting the calamari to one side.
9. Add number four, the shrimp and cook for 6-7 minutes (depending on their size), remove from the pan and set to one side.
10. Add the fifth fish, the scallops, cooking for 5 minutes and remove and setting them to one side.
11. Next is the sixth fish; the scungilli, cook for 45-50 minutes, remove from the pot and put to one side.

12. Finally, add the seventh fish; put the octopus in a colander, and dip the colander in and out a few times. Allow the octopus to cook for approximately 20 minutes, remove and put to one side.

13. When the fish is sufficiently cool, shred the baccala, slice the scungilli and cut the octopus into pieces.

14. In a large mixing bowl, add the mussels along with the calamari, scallops, shrimp, shredded baccala, sliced scungilli and pieces of octopus.

15. Mix all seven fishes together to combine fully.

16. Next, add the vegetables; parsley, celery, carrots, and green olives to the bowl and stir to combine.

17. Next, make the salad dressing by adding all 7 of the dressing ingredients to the bowl; lemon juice, olive oil, garlic cloves, white wine vinegar, a pinch of oregano and red pepper flakes and salt to taste. Stir well to combine.

18. Cover and transfer the bowl to the refrigerator to marinate overnight.

19. Enjoy.

(4)_Anchovies in a Lemon Marinade - Acciughe al Limone

A lot of people enjoy eating anchovies when they are fresh and conserved in salt they are full of flavor. Italian anchovies are plump, full of flavor and among the very best in the world. This recipe combines salt and citrus for the perfect pairing.

Serving Size: 4
Preparation Time: 15mins
Total Cooking Time: 24hours 15mins
Ingredient List:

- ¾ pound anchovies
- Freshly squeezed lemon juice (to taste)
- Salt
- Vinegar
- Oregano (chopped)
- Extra virgin olive oil

Methods:

1. First, clean and scale the anchovies before washing them under cold running tap water. Pat dry.
2. Arrange the anchovies in a baking dish or terrine and generously cover them with freshly squeezed lemon juice, sprinkle with salt and a dash of vinegar and scatter with oregano.
3. Allow the anchovies to marinate for one full day.
4. Drain, and place on a serving platter.
5. Season well and drizzle with olive oil.

(5)_Salmon Canapés

The perfect finger food; simple to make, and quick to prepare which means you get to spend less time in the kitchen and more time with your guests. Plus, light salmon canapés are the perfect way to take a break from some of the meat-laden indulgences of the holiday season.

Serving Size: 8
Preparation Time: 5mins
Cook Time: N/A
Total Cooking Time: 5mins
Ingredient List:

- ¼ English cucumber (cut into 8 slices*)
- 8 whole-wheat crackers
- 4 ounces spreadable herb cheese (room temperature)
- 4 ounces smoked salmon (thinly sliced)
- Red onion (peeled, thinly sliced into rings)

- 3 sprigs fresh parsley
- 1 green onion (thinly sliced on the bias)

Methods:
1. Arrange the slices of cucumber and whole-wheat crackers, on a sandwich platter.
2. Transfer the herb cheese into a piping bag fitted with a star tip.
3. Pipe the cheese in swirls on top of the slices of cucumber and in the center of each cracker.
4. Put the slices of salmon in the shape of a rose over the cheese and garnish with slices of red onion, parsley, and green onion slices.

*Cut the slices of cucumber sufficiently thick enough that you can pick them up.

(6)_Baby Octopus Salad

A cold octopus salad for the second course of the feast is a perfect way to move on into the more hearty courses. This baby octopus salad is dressed with a zesty lemon parsley dressing.

Serving Size: 4
Preparation Time: 20mins
Cook Time: 40mins
Total Cooking Time: 1hour
Ingredient List:

- 2 pounds baby octopus
- 3 medium carrots (coarsely chopped)
- 1 medium onion (peeled, quartered)
- 3 ribs celery (chopped)
- 1 whole lemon (seeded, cut in half)
- Juice of 1 whole lemon
- ¼ cup extra virgin olive oil
- 1 bunch fresh parsley
- ¼ teaspoons salt

- Pepper
- Lettuce (to serve)

Methods:

1. In a large pot filled with cold water, add the octopus along with the carrots, onion, celery and two halves of lemon. Bring to boil, before lowering the heat to a simmer and cooking for 40 minutes.

2. Take the baby octopus out of the pot and discard the pot's contents.

3. Take a sharp knife, and carefully chop the octopus into small pieces, taking care not to chop too finely.

4. In a mixing bowl, whisk the lemon juice into a ¼ cup of olive oil, until the liquid becomes emulsified. Add the parsley and season to taste, stirring to combine.

5. Lay crisp lettuce onto a serving plate and arrange the octopus on top.

6. Drizzle generously with the lemon vinaigrette.

(7)_Tuna Canapés - Tartine al Tonno

The tradition of eating fish on Christmas Eve originates from the Roman Catholic custom of abstaining from meat and dairy products on the eve of certain holidays, including Christmas.

Tartine al Tonno is basically an open-faced sandwich on buttered bread, topped with tuna, egg, capers and pearl onions.

Serving Size: 4-6
Preparation Time: 10mins
Cook Time: N/A
Total Cooking Time: 10mins
Ingredient List:

- 3 ounces canned tuna in oil (drained, flaked)
- 1 hard-boiled egg (shelled, chopped)
- 1 + ½ teaspoons capers
- 1-ounce pickled pearl onions (drained)
- 1-ounce butter (room temperature)
- Juice of 1 medium lemon (seeded, strained)
- Extra virgin olive oil (to drizzle)

- 6 slices white sandwich bread (no crusts)
- Salt
- 1 pickled pepper (cut into thin strips, to garnish)
- 3 ounces green olives (pitted, sliced into rings, to garnish)

Methods:
1. Put the tuna along with the capers and onions in a food blender and blend until a puree.
2. In a small mixing bowl, cream the butter.
3. Push the egg through a metal sieve into the mixing bowl and combine with the puree.
4. Add the lemon juice, beating to fully combine, and season well with salt. Sprinkle in olive oil. Beat the mixture until incorporated.
5. Cut the bread slice in half and, using a blunt knife spread with the tuna mixture.
6. Garnish each piece with pickled pepper strips and olives.

(8)_Shrimp Cocktail - Cocktail di Gamberetti

Shrimp Cocktail is a popular Italian and elegant way to start a holiday feast. This version is prepared in the Italian way. Instead of being made with ketchup and horseradish this Shrimp Cocktail is spooned onto a bed of crisp lettuce and garnished with salmon roe.

Serving Size: 3
Preparation Time: 10mins
Total Cooking Time: 50mins
Ingredient List:

- Cocktail sauce:
- 3½ ounces full-fat mayonnaise
- 1-2 tablespoons ketchup
- Dash of Worcestershire sauce
- 2-3 drops brandy
- Salt and pepper
- Fresh cream

Shrimp:

- ½ pound pre-cooked shrimp

To serve:
- <u>Lettuce</u>
- Salmon Roe
- Fresh parsley (minced)
- 3 whole cooked shrimps (for garnish)
- 3 thin slices lemon (for garnish)

Methods:

1. First, prepare the cocktail sauce: In a mixing bowl briskly combine the mayonnaise, along with the ketchup, Worcestershire sauce, 2 drops of brandy, and a dash of salt and pepper. The cocktail sauce should ideally be pourable and not too thick. If it is a little thick, add a couple of drops of fresh cream to thin the sauce out.

2. Taste the sauce and season accordingly, adding another dash of brandy if needed.

3. If the shrimp are large, using a sharp kitchen knife, cut the shrimp into bite-sized pieces.

4. Add the shrimp to the bowl with the cocktail sauce, and carefully fold the shrimp into the cocktail sauce, using an angled spatula.

5. Cover the bowl with plastic wrap and transfer to the refrigerator for 30-40 minutes.

6. Arrange a couple of crisp lettuce leaves in individual bowls.

7. Evenly divide the shrimp mixture between 3 bowls, and heap it on top of the lettuce. Top with salmon roe and garnish with fresh parsley. Decorate the rim of each glass with a cooked shrimp and a slice of lemon.

8. Serve chilled.

(9)_Italian Seafood Salad – Insalata di Mare

This seafood salad with calamari, mussels, and shrimp is the perfect way to begin an Italian Christmas Eve meal. It's sufficiently light enough to begin the feast and sets the stage for the remaining five courses to follow.

Serving Size: 4
Preparation Time: 20mins
Cook Time: 1hour 20mins
Total Cooking Time: 4hours 40mins
Ingredient List:

- 1¼ cups calamari (cleaned, cut)
- 1½ cups mussels (no shell)
- 1¾ cups small shrimp (cleaned)
- 1 stalk celery (chopped)
- 1 medium carrot (grated)
- 5-6 black olives (chopped)

- ¼ cup Italian parsley (chopped)
- ¼ cup olive oil
- Juice of ½ lemon
- Salt (to taste)
- Balsamic vinegar (to taste)
- Italian bread (to serve)

Methods:

1. In a large pan of boiling water, boil the chopped calamari, for 55-60 minutes. Using a slotted spoon, remove the calamari to a medium mixing bowl.

2. Keep the pan of boiling water and add the mussels, cooking for 10 minutes, remove the mussels to the bowl containing the calamari and add the small shrimp to the boiling water and boil for a further 10 minutes. Remove to the same bowl.

3. Drain the fish in the medium mixing bowl another time to remove any excess liquid and set to one side to cool.

4. Add the celery together with the carrot, olives, parsley, olive oil and freshly squeezed lemon juice. Carefully, mix to incorporate.

5. Transfer to the fridge for 2-3 hours to combine the flavors.

6. Before you are ready to serve add additional olive oil (approx. ¼ of a cup), season with salt, and add the balsamic vinegar.

7. Serve with Italian bread.

(10)_Italian Salt Cod Salad - Insalata di Baccalà

Nonna's most cherished recipe. Italian cod salad is a traditional peasant-style dish served at the Feast of the Seven Fishes throughout homes on Christmas Eve. It is perfect for sharing and is the most famous dish for southern Italians as it reminds them of their humble ancestry.

Serving Size: 4
Preparation Time: 15mins
Cook Time: 8mins
Total Cooking Time: 25mins
Ingredient List:

- 2 pounds cod (hydrated, de-boned) *
- 1 medium carrot (halved)
- 2 large ribs celery (thinly sliced crosswise)
- 1 medium onion (peeled, quartered)
- 1 cup Kalamata olives (pitted)

- Small bunch flat leaf parsley (leaves picked over, finely chopped)
- 1¼ cups extra virgin olive oil
- Salt

Methods:
1. Cut the hydrated fish into pieces of 2x2".
2. In a large pan of water, add the carrots, celery, and onion.
3. As soon as the water comes to simmer, add the pieces of fish and cook for 5-6 minutes, or until the fish begins to flake with a fork.
4. Once the fish is sufficiently cooked, remove any skin and bones. Break the cod up and arrange in a salad bowl along with the Kalamata olives, chopped parsley, olive oil and season with salt to taste. Mix to combine.
5. Transfer the salad to the fridge or serve.

*If you can't source hydrated cod then you can use dry salted cod. To prepare dry salted cod, soak in a bowl of cold water for 48 hours, draining the water 3-4 times every day.

Chapter 2: Roasted, Fried and Hearty

(11)_Whole-Roasted Fennel and Onion Branzino

Branzino is a silver-skinned fish found in abundance in the Medditrannean sea and saltwater lakes. It's firm yet delicate white meat is showcased in this recipe, which sees it whole-roasted with fennel, onion and a splash of white wine. Do not worry if you cannot find branzino easily; you can substitute it for sea bass or red snapper.

Serving Size: 8-10
Preparation Time: 10mins
Cook Time: 30mins
Total Cooking Time: 40mins
Ingredient List:

- ½ cup + 2 tablespoons olive oil
- 3 pounds yellow onion (thinly sliced)
- 3 pounds fennel (sliced, reserve fronds)
- ¼ cup dry white wine
- 3 tablespoons fresh thyme (finely chopped)
- Fresh juice and zest of 1 large orange
- 6 whole fresh branzino fish (cleaned)
- Sea salt and black pepper

Methods:
1. Preheat the main oven to 350 degrees F.
2. In a 12" skillet, heat ½ a cup of oil over a moderately high heat.
3. Add the sliced onions and fennel, sauté for 8-9 minutes, until soft.
4. Toss in the reserved fronds, white wine, chopped thyme and orange juice and zest. Cook for 5-6 minutes.
5. Season the branzino with sea salt and black pepper and then use a ¼ cup of the onion mixture to stuff into the cavities of the fish.
6. Tie fishes' mouths closed using kitchen twine.
7. Add the remaining onion mixture into a roasting pan and rest the fish on top.
8. Drizzle over the 2 tablespoons of oil and place in the oven.
9. Roast for half an hour, until cooked through.

(12)_Crumb-Topped Baked Clams – Vongole al Forno

There are a number of different verities of clams in Italy and Littleneck clams or Cherrystone/Steamer clams as they are also known by are easy to source from local fishmongers. Al Forno is food that has been baked in an oven and Vongole al Forno is always a bit hit, not to mention simple and easy to make leaving you plenty of time to prepare your remaining courses!

Serving Size: 24
Preparation Time: 10mins
Cook Time: 9mins
Total Cooking Time: 20mins
Ingredient List:

- 2 pounds sea salt
- 24 Littleneck clams
- ½ cup breadcrumbs (dry)
- ¼ cup chicken stock
- 1 tablespoon fresh parsley (minced)

- 2 tablespoons olive oil
- 2 cloves garlic (minced)
- ¼ teaspoons dried oregano
- Pinch black pepper
- 1 tablespoon panko breadcrumbs
- Lemon wedges (for serving)

Methods:
1. Spread the salt over an ovenproof serving platter.
2. Shuck the clams, leaving juices and clams in the bottom shells.
3. Arrange the shucked clams on the salted platter, dividing the juices between the shells.
4. Preheat the broiler.
5. In a clean bowl, add the dry bread crumbs, chicken stock, minced parsley, olive oil, minced garlic, dried oregano and black pepper. Mix until combined and spoon evenly over the clams.
6. Place the platter in the oven 6" away from the heat and broil for 7-9 minutes.
7. Serve straight away with lemon wedges.

(13)_Slow Roasted Salmon in Lemon Oil

Sometimes the most straightforward dishes can be the tastiest. This recipe uses few ingredients to allow the fresh fillet of salmon to be the star of the show, allowing all of its natural flavor to shine through. What's more, it's a fuss-free process, allowing you more time to spend on some of your more fiddly dishes.

Serving Size: 8
Preparation Time: 10mins
Cook Time: 10mins
Total Cooking Time: 20mins
Ingredient List:

- 2½ pounds fresh salmon (skin on)
- Sea salt and black pepper
- 1 cup virgin olive oil
- 1 fresh lemon (sliced thinly)
- 6 sprigs fresh thyme

Methods:

1. Preheat the main oven to 300 degrees F.
2. Season the salmon on both sides with sea salt and black pepper.
3. Place the fish in a large baking dish.
4. Drizzle over the olive oil and scatter over the sliced lemon.
5. Arrange the sprigs of time around the fish.
6. Roast in the oven until just cooked, this should take just under 30 minutes.
7. Serve immediately.

(14)_Fritto Misto

Fritto Misto roughly translates to mixed fry. It's a yummy assortment of fried goodies ranging from meat to vegetables. However, on Christmas Eve it should be a strictly seafood affair with fresh sardines, shrimp, scallops, and calamari.

A super light batter stops this dish from being too heavy, while tartar sauce works well as a punchy side for dipping.

Serving Size: 6-8
Preparation Time: 10mins
Cook Time: 10mins
Total Cooking Time: 20mins
Ingredient List:

- 6 cups canola oil
- 2 cups all-purpose flour
- 16 fresh sardines (heads removed)
- 1-pound fresh shrimp (peeled, veined, butterflied)
- 1-pound fresh scallops

- 1-pound fresh calamari
- Sea salt and black pepper
- 3 fresh lemons (sliced into wedges, for serving)
- Tartar sauce (for serving)

Methods:
1. Pour 3" of oil into a skillet and place over moderately high heat, until it reaches 350 degrees F.
2. Sprinkle the flour onto a large plate.
3. Season all of the seafood generously with sea salt and black pepper.
4. Dredge the seafood in flour before dropping in the oil. Fry all of the seafood in batches, until cooked through and golden*.
5. Use a slotted spoon to remove the cooked pieces from the oil and set them aside on a paper towel-lined plate.
6. Transfer the fried fish to a serving plate along with the lemon wedges and tartar sauce.

*Approximately 20 seconds each side for sardines and shrimp, 15 seconds each side for calamari and scallops.

(15)_Seared Scallops with Herby Citrus Sauce

Perfectly browned scallops are delicate yet meaty. A zesty and refreshing sauce made with citrus and herbs helps to enhance their unique flavor. Wilted spinach cooked with a little lemon and garlic will work as a great side dish if you are looking to make a heartier meal for your third course.

Serving Size: 4
Preparation Time: 10mins
Cook Time: 10mins
Total Cooking Time: 20mins
Ingredient List:

- 1½ pounds fresh scallops
- ½ teaspoons sea salt
- ½ teaspoons black pepper
- ¼ teaspoons sweet paprika
- 6 tablespoons salted butter
- 1 clove garlic (minced)

- 2 tablespoons sherry
- 1 tablespoon freshly squeezed lemon juice
- ¼ teaspoons fresh oregano (minced)
- ¼ teaspoons fresh tarragon (minced)

Methods:
1. Pat dry the scallops using kitchen paper towel.
2. Arrange on a plate and sprinkle with the sea salt, black pepper, and paprika.
3. In a heavy skillet, melt 2 tablespoons of salted butter on a moderately high heat.
4. Place the scallops in the skillet and sauté for a couple of minutes each side.
5. Take out of the skillet and set aside on a paper towel-lined plate. Keep warm.
6. In the remaining butter, sauté the garlic until soft. Pour in the sherry and stir.
7. When most of the liquid has evaporated, add the lemon juice and herbs. Stir well.
8. Arrange the scallops on a serving plate and drizzle over the sauce.

(16)_Housewife Style Jumbo Shrimp Marsala - Gamberoni Alla Casalinga Siciliana

A rustic and authentic meal, packed with flavor thanks to the pine nuts, currants, capers, fennel and Marsala wine! This dish makes a perfect third course, which should traditionally be a more substantial 'meaty' offering.

Serving Size: 10-12
Preparation Time: 10mins
Cook Time: 9mins
Total Cooking Time: 20mins
Ingredient List:

- ¼ cup virgin olive oil
- 1 red onion (diced)
- 1 stalk celery (chopped)
- 4 plum tomatoes (chopped roughly)
- 1 tablespoon pine nuts
- 1 cup dry Marsala wine
- 2 tablespoons capers

- ½ teaspoons red pepper flakes
- 1 fresh bay leaf
- 1 tablespoon currants
- ½ teaspoons fennel seeds
- 2 pounds fresh jumbo shrimp (peeled, deveined)
- Sea salt and black pepper

Methods:
1. In an 11" sauté pan, add the olive oil. On a moderately high heat, cook the oil until nearly smoking.
2. Add the diced onion and celery; sauté until soft.
3. Add the plum tomatoes, pine nuts, Marsala wine, capers, red pepper, bay leaf, currants and fennel seeds. Bring the mixture to a boil.
4. Take the pan off the heat and arrange the jumbo shrimp on top of the sauce in a single layer. Cover and simmer on a low heat for 4-5 minutes.
5. Take off the heat, season to taste with sea salt and black pepper. Recover and allow to stand for 5-6 minutes.
6. Serve warm.

(17)_Seafood Stuffed Salmon Fillets

If you're looking to impress, then this seafood stuffed salmon dish is a must-make! And there's no need to panic, although this recipe may look complicated and fancy it's perfectly straightforward to prepare.

Serving Size: 12
Preparation Time: 10mins
Cook Time: 10mins
Total Cooking Time: 20mins
Ingredient List:

- 1½ cups cooked white rice
- 8 ounces crabmeat
- 2 tablespoons full-fat cream cheese (room temperature)
- 2 tablespoons salted butter (melted)
- 2 cloves garlic (minced)
- ½ teaspoons each dried marjoram, basil, thyme, oregano, rosemary, celery seeds (ground)
- 12 (8 ounce) salmon filets

- 3 tablespoons virgin olive oil
- 2 teaspoons dill weed
- 1½ teaspoons sea salt

Methods:

1. Preheat the main oven to 400 degrees F. Grease 2 baking tins and set aside.
2. In a mixing bowl, add the cooked rice, crabmeat, cream cheese, melted butter, minced garlic and dried herbs (marjoram, basil, thyme, oregano, rosemary, and celery seeds).
3. Carefully slice a horizontal pocket into each fillet and stuff with the rice cream cheese mixture. Use toothpicks to secure if necessary.
4. Arrange the salmon in the baking tins, brush with more oil and sprinkle over the dill weed and sea salt.
5. Place in the oven and roast for approximately 20 minutes.
6. Remove the toothpicks and serve!

(18)_Oven Roasted Baccala with Potatoes

There aren't many guidelines when it comes to what you should prepare for your feast, but many families would agree that serving baccala for at least one of your courses is an unwritten rule. For some, the flavor of this dry salted codfish can be a little unusual. However, the sweet flavor of the onions and roasted potatoes prevent the flavor of the fish from overpowering the dish.

Serving Size: 8
Preparation Time: 10mins
Cook Time: 30mins
Total Cooking Time: 40mins
Ingredient List:

- 1¼ pounds prepared baccala fish*
- 2 potatoes (thinly sliced into rounds)
- 1 medium yellow onion (thinly sliced)
- 3 tablespoons salted butter (chilled, chopped)
- ¼ cup + extra virgin olive oil

- Pinch red pepper flakes
- Black pepper

Methods:
1. Preheat the main oven to 375 degrees F.
2. Rinse the baccala and chop into small pieces.
3. Toss together the sliced potatoes and onions in the butter and ¼ cup olive oil in a shallow casserole dish.
4. Add in the chopped baccala and toss again.
5. Season with red pepper flakes and a small pinch of black pepper.
6. Cover the dish with aluminum foil and place in the oven.
7. Roast for approximately half an hour, if needed add a drop or two of water as it's cooking. Taste and season with a pinch of salt if necessary.
8. Serve straight away with a drizzle of olive oil.

*The baccala must be prepared and soaked at least 3 days before cooking the dish.

(19)_Sea Bass Alla Fiorentina

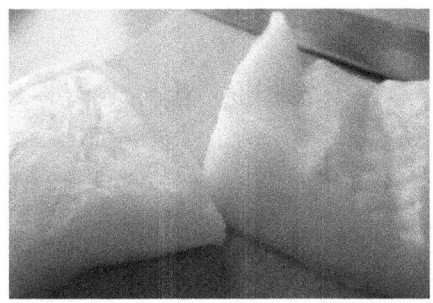

Coated with a super light and delicate salt and pepper batter, this heavenly sea bass dish straight from Florence, is a real crowd pleaser. Serve on top of a fresh and fruity tomato sauce made with Italian herbs and garlic.

Serving Size: 4
Preparation Time: 10mins
Cook Time: 20mins
Total Cooking Time: 30mins
Ingredient List:

- Sea salt and black pepper
- 4 (6 ounce) sea bass pieces
- 2 cups all-purpose flour
- 6 teaspoons virgin olive oil
- 3 cloves garlic (finely chopped)
- 14 ounces canned crushed tomatoes
- ½ cup water

- 1 tablespoon fresh parsley (chopped)
- 1 tablespoon fresh basil (chopped)
- ¼ teaspoons sea salt
- ½ teaspoons black pepper

Methods:
1. Sprinkle sea salt and black pepper on both sides of each piece of fish.
2. In a shallow bowl, add the flour. Dip each fish in the bowl of flour, tapping off any excess.
3. Set the fish aside on a plate for a moment.
4. In a medium frying pan, heat 3 tablespoons of olive oil. Place the fish in the pan and sauté for a few minutes each side. Return the fish to the plate for a moment.
5. Wipe the pan clean and pour in the remaining olive oil. When the oil is hot, add the chopped garlic, crushed tomatoes, water and chopped parsley, sea salt, and pepper. Simmer for 10 minutes before adding the basil and fish. Cook for 2 minutes before serving immediately.

(20)_Sautéed Sole with Olive Tapenade

Dover sole has a firm yet fluffy texture and mild flavor, making it the perfect fish base for a punchy green and black olive topping with balsamic vinegar, anchovies and capers. Oven roasted potatoes would go brilliantly with this light yet hearty dish.

Serving Size: 8
Preparation Time: 10mins
Cook Time: 10mins
Total Cooking Time: 20mins
Ingredient List:

- ⅓ cup virgin olive oil
- ¼ cup Kalamata olives (pitted)
- ¼ cup green olives (pitted)
- 2 tablespoons fresh parsley (finely chopped)
- 1 tablespoon garlic (finely chopped)
- 1 tablespoon good quality balsamic vinegar
- 2 teaspoons tinned capers (rinsed)
- 2 tinned anchovy fillets

- 1 plum tomato (chopped)
- Sea salt and black pepper
- 8 (4 ounce) fresh Dover sole fillets

Methods:

1. Into a food processor, add 2 tablespoons virgin olive oil, the Kalamata and green olives, chopped parsley and garlic, balsamic vinegar, capers, anchovy fillets, chopped tomato, sea salt and black pepper.
2. Pulse until finely chopped and set aside.
3. In a 12" skillet, heat the remaining oil and cook the sole over a moderately high heat for 5 minutes, until cooked through.
4. Arrange the fillets on a serving platter, and top with the olive mixture.
5. Serve straight away.

Chapter 3: Pasta and Stew

(21)_Umbrian Fish Stew

A traditional bouillabaisse-like fish stew made with tomatoes and freshwater fish. Umbrian cuisine is rustic and is a peasant style of cooking, meaning it is based on traditional dishes, made with local produce including freshwater fish such as pike, carp, perch, and tench.

Serving Size: 6
Preparation Time: 20mins
Cook Time: 25mins
Total Cooking Time: 45mins
Ingredient List:
For the soup:

- 2-pound mixed freshwater fish fillets (cut into 2" pieces)
- ½ teaspoons salt

- ½ cup onion (peeled, chopped)
- ½ cup celery (chopped)
- 4 cloves garlic (finely chopped)
- ¼ cup flat-leaf parsley (chopped)
- 1 cup Trebbiano white wine
- 1 (28-ounce) can crushed Italian tomatoes
- 2 cups water
- 1 teaspoon salt

For the toasts:
- 1 Italian baguette
- 1 clove garlic
- 2 tablespoons extra-virgin olive oil

Garnish:
- <u>Flat-leaf parsley (chopped)</u>

Methods:
1. First, make the soup: Pat the fish dry and sprinkle with salt.
2. In a frying pan or skillet, over moderate heat, cook the onion along with the celery, and garlic, occasionally stirring, until the onion is soft but not brown, this will take around 6-8 minutes.
3. Add the chopped parsley and cook, while stirring for 60 seconds.
4. Pour in the Trebbiano and boil until the liquid reduces by 50%, about 5 minutes.
5. Add the crushed tomatoes, 2 cups of water, and the salt and bring to simmer. Add the fish pieces and

reduce the heat, and cook at just simmer for 10 minutes, or until the fish is cooked through.

6. In the meantime, make the toast. Preheat your broiler.

7. Using a sharp bread knife, cut 18 slices from the baguette of around ½" thick. Toast the slices 3-5" away from the heat, flipping over once until the bread is golden brown, 3-4 minutes.

8. Chop the clove of garlic into 2 and run the cut sides on the toasts, and lightly brush with olive oil.

9. Garnish the soup with chopped parsley and serve with the garlic toast.

(22)_Linguine with Tuna Puttanesca

Create an Italian inspired dish, fit for a feast in under half an hour by tossing together these simple ingredients. This dish has a colorful past, it is famously named after Italy's 'ladies of the night' who, it is said very quickly made it in between clients!

Serving Size: 4
Preparation Time: 15mins
Cook Time: 12mins
Total Cooking Time: 27mins
Ingredient List:

- Kosher salt
- 12 ounces linguine
- 2 tablespoons extra virgin olive oil
- 4 garlic cloves (thinly sliced)
- ½ teaspoons red pepper flakes
- 2 tablespoons capers (drained)
- ½ cup Kalamata olives (roughly chopped)
- 1 (28 ounce) can Italian plum tomatoes

- 4 basil leaves (torn)
- 1 (5 ounce) can albacore tuna in olive oil
- Ground black pepper
- Basil leaves (to garnish)

Methods:

1. Fill a large pan with water, add salt and bring to boil. Add the linguine pasta and cook until the linguine is al dente.
2. In the meantime, over moderate heat, heat the olive oil in a large frying pan or skillet.
3. Add the sliced garlic along with the red pepper flakes and while stirring, cook until just toasted, this will take around 1-2 minutes.
4. Next, add the drained capers and Kalamata olives and sauté for another 2 minutes.
5. Put the tomatoes in a bowl, and using clean hands, pick up and crush the plum tomatoes into the pan, setting aside the juices.
6. Cook until the crushed tomatoes are a just dry, for 2-3 minutes. Add the juices reserved earlier, along with the torn basil and a pinch of kosher salt to season and cook until the sauce begins to thicken, 2 minutes.
7. Add the tuna together with the olive oil and using a metal fork break it up. Season again with a pinch of salt.
8. Drain the linguine, reserving ½ cup of the pasta water, and returning the linguine to the pot. Add the sauce and the reserved water and toss.
9. Season and garnish with basil.

(23)_Tuscan Seafood Stew – Cacciucco

One of the unique points of this Tuscan stew is that it is ladled over croutons. The toasted bread soaks up the light and flavorsome broth. Legend says that traditional Cacciucco is made up of five different types of fish or seafood, one for each letter 'c' in its name. It was the fisherman's way of using up any leftover catch in the bottom of his boat.

Serving Size: 5-6
Preparation Time: 5mins
Cook Time: 20mins
Total Cooking Time: 25mins
Ingredient List:

- 1 (12 slice) loaf artisan bread
- Cooking spray
- 1 teaspoon garlic powder
- 1 teaspoon olive oil
- 2 medium onions (peeled, diced)
- 4 cloves garlic (minced)

- 6 celery stalks (diced)
- 2 tablespoons parsley
- 2 teaspoons sage
- 1 teaspoon red pepper flakes
- 4 tomatoes (finely diced)
- 1½ cups water
- ¼ cup red wine vinegar
- 1 teaspoon salt
- 3 pounds mixed fish or seafood *(cut into bite-sized pieces)

Methods:

1. Preheat the main oven to 275 degrees F.
2. Cut the slices of bread into 1" cubes and place the cubes on a baking tray or sheet.
3. Lightly mist the cubes of bread with cooking spray and sprinkle garlic powder over the cubes.
4. Toast in the preheated oven for 20 minutes, or until the bread is dry.
5. In a large soup pot, heat the oil and add the onions along with the garlic, celery, parsley, sage and red pepper flakes and fry over moderate heat until the onions are soft around 5 minutes.
6. Add the diced tomatoes along with the water, red wine vinegar, and salt and bring to simmer.
7. Chop the fish/seafood into bite-sized pieces and add to the soup. Simmer until the fish/seafood is sufficiently cooked through, 12-15 minutes.
8. Arrange the croutons in the bottom of individual bowls and ladle the stew over the top.

(24)_Lobster Fra Diavolo

When you want to make an impression serve this opulent lobster pasta dish. Fra Diavolo translates as devil-monk, which is the name given to spicy sauce for seafood or pasta. This dish is mostly reserved for special occasions and holiday feast.

Serving Size: 4-6
Preparation Time: 25mins
Cook Time: 40mins
Total Cooking Time: 1hour 5mins
Ingredient List:

- 3 tablespoons olive oil
- 1 medium onion (peeled, finely chopped)
- 2 garlic cloves (finely chopped)
- 1 cup Italian dry white wine
- 3 cups chopped, canned Italian tomatoes
- Salt and pepper
- 2 tablespoons fresh basil (finely chopped)

- Red pepper flakes
- 2 (1½ pound) lobsters
- 1-pound fresh linguine
- 3 tablespoons fresh parsley (finely chopped)

Methods:
1. In a large saucepan, heat the oil.
2. Add the onions to the pan and cook until translucent and softened, next add the chopped garlic.
3. Cook the garlic for 60-90 seconds, or until it emits its fragrance.
4. Add the dry white wine and cook until the liquid reduces by half.
5. Next, add the canned tomatoes and stir to combine.
6. Season with salt and pepper. Sprinkle in the fresh basil and add a dash of red pepper flakes.
7. Cook for 12-15 minutes over a low heat.
8. Cut each of the lobster in half, across their length, and add to the sauce.
9. Cook for 15-20 minutes over low heat, until they are bright pink and the lobster meat is sufficiently cooked.
10. Remove the lobster from the sauce and cut the lobster meat from the claws and the tail and cut into bite-sized pieces.
11. Return the lobster meat to the sauce and keep warm.
12. In the meantime, and while the lobster is cooking, add salted water to a pot and bring to boil.
13. Add the linguine and cook until al dente.
14. Drain the linguine and return it to the pot.

15. Add 2-3 ladles of the sauce to the linguine and over moderate heat, stir well to combine.
16. Evenly divide the linguine into 4 pasta bowls and top with the remaining sauce.
17. Sprinkle parsley over the top and serve.

(25)_Squid Ink Seafood Pasta

A light pasta dish is perfect for your Seven Fishes family celebration. Squid ink pasta adds color and gives a salty yet sweet flavor to the tagliatelle. If you enjoy, fried calamari try experimenting with other squid dishes. The secret is to cook the squid quickly either high and hot or slow and low.

Serving Size: 6-8
Preparation Time: 10mins
Cook Time: 25mins
Total Cooking Time: 35mins
Ingredient List:

- 1-pound squid and tentacles
- 4 tablespoons extra virgin olive oil
- 2 small shallots (finely chopped)
- 3 garlic cloves (minced)
- 3 teaspoons salt + 1 tablespoon for the pasta water
- 1 teaspoon black pepper
- 1 (12 ounce) can plum tomatoes

- ¼ cup Pinot Grigio
- 1-pound squid ink tagliatelle pasta

Methods:
1. First, using a sharp knife slice the body of the squid into ¼" rings and mix with the squid's tentacles.
2. In a large frying pan, heat the olive oil over a moderate to low heat.
3. Add the chopped shallots, and fry until translucent, 2-3 minutes.
4. Add the squid, and cook for 60 seconds, or until they become light pink.
5. Add the garlic to the pan along with the salt, and black pepper and fry for 3-4 minutes.
6. Add the tomatoes along with the Pinot Grigio and allow to simmer for a few minutes.
7. Turn the heat off, cover the pan, and set to one side.
8. Bring a large pan of boiling salted water to boil and cook the pasta for between 3-4 minutes, if you are using fresh pasta, or 8-9 if dried.
9. Transfer the pasta to the pan along with the sauce, toss to evenly combine and serve.

(26)_Nonna's Cioppino

Bursting with fresh seafood in a tomato and white wine broth with flavors of the sea, Cioppino is a favorite Italian-American stew. Cioppino is a fish stew originally hailing from San Francisco in California and is related to various regional Italian fish soups and stews.

Serving Size: 4
Preparation Time: 30mins
Cook Time: 1hour
Total Cooking Time: 1hour 30mins
Ingredient List:

- 3 tablespoons virgin olive oil
- 3 large shallots (chopped)
- 1 large fennel bulb (thinly sliced)
- 1 medium yellow onion (peeled, chopped)
- 2 teaspoons salt
- 4 large cloves garlic (finely chopped)
- ¾ teaspoons dried/crushed red pepper flakes
- ¼ cup tomato paste

- 1 (28 ounce) canned tomatoes (diced in juice)
- 5 cups fish stock
- 12 ounces Italian dry white wine
- 1 fresh bay leaf
- 1-pound mussels (scrubbed, debearded)
- 1-pound manila clams (thoroughly scrubbed)
- 1-pound large uncooked shrimp (peeled, deveined)
- 1½ pounds fish fillets (cut into 3" chunks) *
- Salt and pepper (to season)

Methods:
1. In an extra large pan or pot, over moderate heat, heat the olive oil.
2. Add the chopped shallots along with the sliced fennel, chopped onion, and 2 teaspoons of salt and fry for 8-10 minutes, or until the onion becomes translucent.
3. Add the finely chopped garlic along with the crushed red pepper flakes, and fry for a couple of minutes.
4. Stir in the tomato paste, mixing well to combine.
5. Pour in the canned tomatoes (and juices) and add the stock, white wine, and fresh bay leaf.
6. Cover the pan and bring to simmer, before reducing to a moderate to low heat. Cover the pan and simmer for 25-30 minutes, to allow the flavors to fuse.
7. Add the mussels along with the manila clams to the liquid and cover. Continue cooking until they are both beginning to open; this will take between 5-6 minutes.
8. Next, add the shrimp together with the fish fillets. Simmer until both are sufficiently cooked, the clams

completely open, and while gently stirring cook for an additional 5 minutes. Make sure you discard any mussels or clams that do not properly open.

9. Season the Cioppino, with additional salt and pepper if needed.

10. Ladle the soup into bowls and serve.

*Halibut and salmon are excellent choices for Cioppino

(27)_Spaghetti with Clams - Spaghetti Alle Vongole

This seafood pasta dish is hugely popular throughout the whole of Italy, especially in Campania. With only six main ingredients this clam pasta is very easy to prepare, yet incredibly tasty; the fresher the clams, the better the taste. Once tried, never forgotten!

Serving Size: 2
Preparation Time: 5mins
Cook Time: 15mins
Total Cooking Time: 20mins
Ingredient List:

- Kosher salt
- 6 ounces spaghetti
- 4 tablespoons extra-virgin oil (divided)
- 1 clove garlic (thinly sliced)
- ¼ teaspoons crushed, dried red pepper flakes
- ¼ cup Italian white wine

- 2 pounds Littleneck or Manila clams (scrubbed)
- 2 tablespoons fresh flat-leaf parsley (roughly chopped)

Methods:

1. Take a pot, with no less capacity than 5 quarts and fill it with 3 quarts of lightly salted water. Bring to boil and add the spaghetti, cook while occasionally stirring for 2 minutes, or until just tender. Drain, the pasta, while setting a ½ cup of pasta cooking water to one side.

2. In the meantime, heat 3 tablespoons of olive oil in a large frying pan or skillet over moderate heat. Add the sliced garlic and sauté, while frequently swirling the skillet until the garlic is golden.

3. Stir in the red pepper flakes and continue frying for 15 seconds.

4. Pour in the white wine, followed by the clams, and increase the temperature to high heat.

5. Cover the skillet and continue cooking until the clams begin to open and release their juices, this will take between 4-6 minutes, depending very much on the actual size of the clams. As soon as the clams open, use kitchen tongs to place them in a mixing bowl.

6. Pour approximately ¼ cup of the pasta water reserved earlier to the skillet and bring to boil. Add the spaghetti to the pan and over high heat, cook while continually tossing. Cook until the spaghetti is al dente and soaked in the sauce from the pan.

7. Add the clams along with any pan juices, to the bowl, sprinkle in the parsley and toss well to combine. If you

feel the sauce is a little too dry add additional pasta cooking water.

8. Divide the pasta between warmed bowls and drizzle with remaining olive oil.

(28)_Salted Cod - Baccala Stew

Salted cod or baccala, nearly always forms part of the Feast of the Seven Fishes. The dish consists of chunks of cod, dredged and fried in flour and braised in a spicy tomato-based sauce. Baccala is a low-cost fish and was, therefore, a popular choice for peasants when times were hard.

Serving Size: 4
Preparation Time: 15mins
Cook Time:40mins
Total Cooking Time: 48hours 55mins
Ingredient List:

- 3 medium potatoes (washed, cut into 2" pieces)
- 1-pound soaked, salted cod*(skin removed)
- ¼ cup all-purpose flour
- 5 tablespoons extra virgin olive oil
- 1 large onion (peeled, chopped)
- 2 stalks celery (finely chopped)

- 1 cup Pinot Gringo
- 1 cup fish stock
- Pinch red chili flakes
- 1 box (26.46 ounces) tomatoes (chopped)
- ¼ cup olives (pitted, chopped)
- 1½ tablespoons capers (chopped)
- Black pepper
- 3 tablespoons fresh parsley (chopped)

Methods:
1. In a pan filled with water, boil the potatoes for 6 minutes. Drain the potatoes and put to one side.
2. Chop the de-skinned cod into pieces, no more than 3-4" in size.
3. Lightly, evenly dust the cod pieces in the flour.
4. In a large pan or pot, over moderate heat, heat the oil. Add the fish to the pan and lightly fry for a couple of minutes on each side, or until just browned. Remove from the pan and put to one side.
5. Add the chopped onion together with the celery to the pan and cook over a moderate heat for 7-8 minutes.
6. Pour in the Pinot Grigio and over high heat, cook until virtually of the liquid has evaporated, this will take between 5-7 minutes.
7. Add the fish stock along with the chili flakes, tomatoes, olives and capers and bring to a fast boil.
8. Next, add the potatoes, and reduce the heat and cook at a simmer for 5 minutes.

9. Return the cod to the pan and season with pepper. Sprinkle with the parsley, cover the pan and simmer for 20 minutes.

10. Serve.

* Soak the cod in a deep bowl filled with cold water for 48 hours, changing the water once every 24 hours.

(29)_Spaghetti with Anchovies - Spaghetti con Acciughe

This particular recipe features as one of the seven dishes served on Christmas Eve. Each region of Italy has its own typical dishes; cod fritters in Naples, Pasta, broccoli and arzilla fish soup in Rome and spaghetti with anchovies in Calabria.

Serving Size: 8
Preparation Time: 15mins
Cook Time: 15mins
Total Cooking Time: 30mins
Ingredient List:

- 1-pound pasta
- 3 tablespoons extra virgin olive oil
- 2 large cloves garlic (chopped)
- 14 ounces anchovy fillets (chopped)
- ½ teaspoons crushed red pepper flakes
- 4 tablespoons dried breadcrumbs

Methods:
1. In a pot of boiling salted water cook the pasta according to the manufacturer's instructions.
2. In a frying pan over moderate heat, heat the olive oil and add the garlic, cooking until it emits its fragrance and begins to brown.
3. Remove the pieces of garlic from the pan and add the anchovies. Using a wooden spoon, mash the anchovies until they dissolve in the oil. Add the crushed red pepper and reduce the heat, cooking for 2-3 minutes.
4. Drain the pasta and top with anchovy sauce.
5. Drizzle with olive oil and scatter with breadcrumbs.

(30)_Sea Bass & Seafood Italian One-Pot

The perfect Mediterranean recipe; a one-pot stew means you can sit down with your family and join in on the Christmas Eve festivities. Serve with crusty Italian bread for mopping up the sauce.

Serving Size: 4
Preparation Time: 15mins
Cook Time: 45mins
Total Cooking Time: 1hour
Ingredient List:

- 2 tablespoons virgin olive oil
- 1 fennel bulb (halved, sliced, fronds reserved for garnish)
- 2 cloves garlic (sliced)
- ½ medium red chili (seeded, chopped)
- 8 ¾ ounces squid (cleaned, sliced into rings)
- Bunch basil (leaves/stalks separated, stalk tied together, leaves roughly chopped)

- 1 (14 ounce) can chopped tomatoes
- 5 ounces Italian white wine
- 2 large handfuls of clams
- 8 raw, large whole prawns
- 4 (5 ounce) sea bass fillets (de-boned)
- Italian crusty bread (to serve)

Methods:
1. In a large pan with a tightly fitting lid, heat the olive oil. Add the sliced fennel along with the sliced garlic and chopped red chili. Sauté until just softened, and then add the squid, basil stalks, chopped tomatoes and white wine. Over low heat, simmer for 30-35 minutes, or until the squid rings are just tender and the mixture has slightly thickened Season with salt and pepper.
2. Scatter the clams and whole prawns evenly over the sauce mixture, arrange the fillets of sea bass on top, and cover with the lid, increase the heat to high and cook for 5 minutes, or until the fish and seafood is cooked right through. The prawns should be pink with red tails, and the flesh opaque, and the sea bass should flake when using a fork.
3. Scatter with fennel fronds and basil leaves.
4. Serve with crusty Italian bread for dipping.

Chapter 4: Palette Cleansers and Desserts

(31)_Sparkling Prosecco Sgroppino

Is it sorbet, is it a cocktail? No-one is quite sure, but it's zesty, refreshing, sparkling with Prosecco, and spiked with a little vodka. A perfect and traditional palette cleansing way to finish a heavy feast and raise a toast to Christmas Eve.

Serving Size: 6
Preparation Time: 5mins
Total Cooking Time: 5mins
Ingredient List:

- 3 cups Prosecco (well chilled)
- 6 tablespoons good quality vodka (well chilled)
- 1 cup lemon sorbet (frozen)

- ¾ teaspoons fresh mint (chopped)

Methods:
1. Take 6 champagne flutes. Into each pour ½ a cup of Prosecco, followed by 1 tablespoon of vodka. Stir gently with a long spoon.
2. Scoop a little lemon sorbet into the glass and finish with a fresh mint garnish.
3. Serve immediately.

(32)_After-Dinner Biscotti

A classic and crunchy Italian biscuit is the perfect accompaniment for after-dinner espresso. This no-frills recipe does not rely on fancy flavors or elaborate fillings, simply a little anise and a few handfuls of chopped almonds; just how Nonna likes to make it!

Serving Size: 30
Preparation Time: 15mins
Cook Time: 35mins

Total Cooking Time: 50mins
Ingredient List:

- 12 ounces salted butter
- 1¾ cups granulated sugar
- 6 medium eggs
- 1 teaspoon anise essence
- 2 teaspoons vanilla essence
- 6 cups all-purpose flour
- ½ teaspoons sea salt
- 2 teaspoons baking powder
- 8 ounces almonds (chopped)

Methods:
1. Preheat the main oven to 350 degrees F.
2. Cream together the butter and granulated sugar in a mixing bowl.
3. Beat in the eggs, one egg at a time, until incorporated and fluffy.
4. Stir in the essences.
5. In a separate mixing bowl, sift the all-purpose flour, with the sea salt, and baking powder.
6. Add the flour mixture to the wet mixture in batches.
7. Fold in the chopped nuts.
8. Work the mixture with your hands until the dough comes together.
9. Split the dough into 4 equal-sized pieces.
10. Roll each piece of dough into a 15" log.
11. Arrange the 4 logs on 2 cookie sheets.
12. Flatten each log gently until approximately 3" wide, with a slight hump down the middle.

13. Place in the oven and bake for just under half an hour.
14. Remove from the oven and slice the logs diagonally, unto ½" wide slices.
15. Rearrange the biscuits on the cookie trays, laying them flat and put back in the oven,
16. Bake for a final 7-9 minutes, turning over halfway through cooking.
17. Allow to cool completely before serving.

(33)_Red Grapefruit and Black Pepper Sorbetto

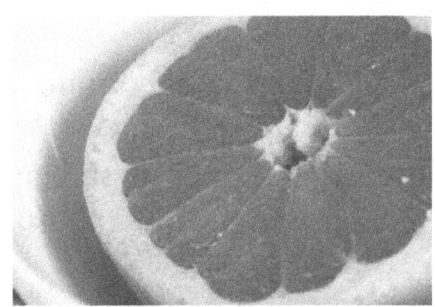

There are no set rules as to what should be served for each course, however, many Italians agree that serving an intermezzo (palette cleanser) before dessert, is a great way to make the transition from savory to sweet courses. This bright and zingy sorbetto, with a black pepper kick, is ideal for cleansing the taste buds ready for the final course.

Serving Size: 6-8
Preparation Time: 10mins
Cook Time: 10mins
Total Cooking Time: 12 hours 45mins
Ingredient List:

- 1¼ cups granulated sugar
- 1¼ cups water
- 1 teaspoon grapefruit zest (grated)
- 2 cups fresh red grapefruit juice
- 2 tablespoons fresh lemon juice

- ½ teaspoons freshly cracked black peppercorns

Methods:

1. In a saucepan, bring to boil the granulated sugar, water, and grated zest. Stir until the sugar has dissolved. Take off the heat and set aside for 5-7 minutes.
2. Add the fresh juices and stir before straining the liquid through a fine-mesh into a clean bowl.
3. Sprinkle with the pepper and stir again. Set to one side to cool before covering and placing in the refrigerator for 5-6 hours.
4. Transfer the refrigerated sorbetto to an ice cream maker and process according to manufacturer's instructions.
5. Finally, scoop the sorbetto into a re-sealable container and freeze for at least 1-2 hours, until ready to serve.

(34)_Chocolate Covered Italian Flag Cookies

What better way to finish off a truly Italian feast, than with adorable and patriotic little flag cookies? Layers of home-baked tri-color almond sponge are sandwiched together with raspberry jam and all coated with a thin layer of dark chocolate. These cookies may be a little time consuming to make, but they are worth it.

Serving Size: 120
Preparation Time: 15mins
Cook Time: 15mins
Total Cooking Time: 3hours 30mins
Ingredient List:

- Butter and flour (for pans)
- 1½ cups unsalted butter (room temperature)
- 1 cup white sugar
- 12½ ounces canned almond pastry filling
- 4 medium eggs
- 2 cups plain flour
- Red food gel (10-12 droplets)
- Green food gel (10-12 droplets)
- 12 ounces raspberry seedless jam
- 12 ounces semisweet choc chips (melted)

Methods:
1. Preheat the main oven to 350 degrees F.
2. Take 3 (9x13") baking tins and grease and flour. Line each with a sheet of parchment and set to one side.
3. Using an electric hand mixer, cream together the butter and white sugar until fluffy and light.
4. Beat in the almond pastry filling.
5. Whisk in the eggs, one at a time, until incorporated.

6. Finally, fold through the flour until just combined, taking care not to over mix.
7. Divide the batter equally into 3 medium bowls.
8. Add approximately 10-12 droplets of red food gel to one bowl and 10-12 droplets of green food gel to another, leaving one bowl of cake batter uncolored. Stir the colored batters well.
9. Transfer each bowl of batter into a prepared baking tin and use a silicone spatula to smooth the surface until even.
10. Bake each cake individually in the oven for 9-11 minutes.
11. Turn the baked cakes out of the tins onto wire racks to cool completely.
12. In the meantime, over medium heat, cook the jam in a 1 quart saucepan until smooth. Set aside to cool a little.
13. Take a cookie sheet and line with aluminum foil. Place the cooled green sponge on the cookie sheet.
14. Use a clean silicon spatula to spread half of the raspberry jam over the top of the green sponge.
15. Arrange the white sponge on top, spread over the remaining jam and sandwich the red sponge on top.
16. Refrigerate the cake for 1-2 hours.
17. Use a sharp knife to trim the rounded edges of the cake, making a sharp-sided rectangular block.
18. Slice the block of cake into 1½" wide strips. Spread the melted chocolate over the top and sides of each block.

19. Cover and return to refrigerator until the chocolate has set.
20. Cut each log into ½" slices and serve.

(35)_Pizzelle Della Nonna

Pizzelle are thin, delicate crispy wafer cookies. First made in Abruzzo in the 8th Century, pizzelle get their shape from the hot iron plates they are flattened between, often these plates would be embossed with a family crest or even snowflake patterns. Pizzelle can be enjoyed all year but in abundance at Christmas time. Many say it would not be a true Christmas Eve feast without them!

Serving Size: 72
Preparation Time: 10mins
Cook Time: 10mins
Total Cooking Time: 20mins
Ingredient List:

- 6 medium eggs
- 1½ cups granulated sugar
- 1 cup salted butter (melted)
- 1 teaspoon lemon zest (grated)
- 1 teaspoon vanilla essence

- 3½ cups all-purpose flour
- 4 teaspoons baking powder

Methods:

1. Beat together the eggs in a mixing bowl, using an electric whisk. When light and foamy, add the granulated sugar, melted butter, grated zest and vanilla essence.
2. Sift through the all-purpose flour and baking powder. Fold through until just combined.
3. Heat your waffle or pizzelle iron.
4. Drop teaspoons of the batter, one at a time onto the center of each patterned well of the iron. Close and heat for approximately 20-40 seconds*
5. Cool the cookies completely on wire baking racks before serving.

*Time will vary greatly, depending on your iron and temperature settings. It's a good idea to set a little batter aside for a few 'test cookies' to work out the perfect cooking time.

(36)_Christmas Fried Honey Fritters – Struffoli

The fondest Christmas memory for many Italians would be munching on these sweet, fried little delights dripping with honey on Christmas Eve. The custom of preparing these festive bites for visitors is said to date back to the 18th Century when the nuns would make struffoli to give as a gift to the nobles of the city.

Serving Size: 30
Preparation Time: 15mins
Cook Time: 15mins
Total Cooking Time: 1hour 20mins
Ingredient List:
Dough:

- 2 cups plain flour
- ¼ teaspoons fine salt
- 3 medium eggs
- 1 teaspoon vanilla essence

- Canola oil

Honey syrup:

- 1 cup clear honey
- ½ cup granulated sugar
- 1 tablespoon fresh lemon juice
- Sprinkles (optional)

Methods:
1. Combine the plain flour, salt, eggs, vanilla essence and canola oil in a large bowl. Knead until you have a smooth dough. Set aside to rest for 25-30 minutes.
2. On a floured surface, roll out the dough into ¼" thick pieces. Cut these pieces into ¼" strips.
3. Roll the strips into thin logs then slice the logs into small pieces (roughly the same size as a hazelnut).
4. Fill a large heavy saucepan a third of the way full of canola oil and heat until it is 'popping.'
5. Use a slotted spoon to place the small dough balls into the oil and deep fry for approximately 2-3 minutes. Remove them with the slotted spoon and rest on kitchen paper towel to remove any excess oil.
6. In a large saucepan, add the honey, granulated sugar, and fresh lemon juice. Bring to a boil over medium heat, stirring until the sugar dissolves.
7. Take off the heat and toss the fried dough balls into the syrup. Stir gently but well until all of the dough balls are coated in the syrup.
8. Allow to cool for a few minutes in the pan before transferring to a serving plate.
9. Scatter with sprinkles if desired and serve warm.

(37)_Limoncello Gelato

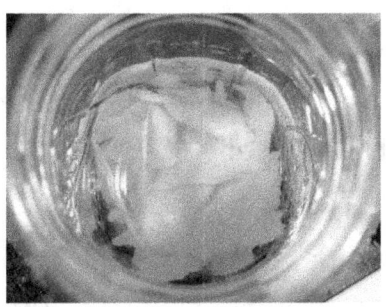

This Southern Italian, lemon-flavored liqueur has been made in homes for over a century with each family having their individual recipe and methods. If you don't have time to make your own, don't worry; it's super easy to find a delicious bottle of Italian produced Limoncello in liquor stores. Grab a bottle and use it in this delicious gelato. Made with mascarpone cheese, fresh lemon peel and vanilla, it's a delightfully creamy yet zesty palette cleanser.

Serving Size: 8
Preparation Time: 10mins
Cook Time: 10mins
Total Cooking Time: 12hours 40mins
Ingredient List:

- 2 cups heavy cream
- ½ cup whole milk
- ¼ cup buttermilk
- ¼ cup mascarpone cheese

- 4 whole coffee beans
- 1 teaspoon fresh lemon peel (grated)
- Scrapings of 1 vanilla bean
- 4 egg yolks
- ½ cup white sugar
- 2 tablespoons freshly squeezed lemon juice
- ¼ cup Italian Limoncello

Methods:

1. In a saucepan, heat together the cream, whole milk, buttermilk, mascarpone cheese, coffee beans and lemon peel. Stir until the mixture begins to bubble at the edges. Take off the heat and cover. Set aside for 15-20 minutes.
2. In the meantime, whisk together the egg yolks, white sugar, and fresh lemon juice.
3. Add the cream mixture to the egg mixture a little at a time, slowly whisking.
4. Transfer the mixture back into the saucepan and return to the heat.
5. Cook on a medium heat, until the mixture thickens and registers 180 degrees F on a candy thermometer, do not boil the mixture,
6. Take off the heat and pour into a mixing bowl. Pour in the Limoncello and stir well.
7. Allow to cool for 4-5 hours, returning at intervals to stir.
8. Add the mixture to an ice cream maker and process according to manufacturer's directions.
9. Transfer to a re-sealable container and freeze for 8-10 hours.

10. Scoop and serve in glasses.

(38)_Candied Christmas Semifreddo with Cherry Liqueur Fruitcake

Semifreddo (translating as half-cold in English) is an iced dessert with a divine creamy mousse-like texture. Thanks to its low water content, it can be much less time consuming to prepare; no ice cream maker or constant churning necessary. Indulgent, without being heavy, this Christmas semifreddo with candied fruit, cherry liqueur and slices of fruitcake is guaranteed to leave your guests satisfied and a happy.

Serving Size: 8
Preparation Time: 15mins
Cook Time: N/A
Total Cooking Time: 5hours 15mins
Ingredient List:

- 4 medium eggs (separated)
- ⅓ cup white sugar

- 1 cup mascarpone cheese
- 1 cup double cream
- 3½ ounces mixed candied fruit (chopped)
- 1 tablespoon cherry liqueur
- 6 medium thick slices fruitcake

Methods:
1. Using a double boiler, heat together the egg yolks and white sugar. Beat until thick and creamy. Take off the heat and set aside for 10-12 minutes.
2. In a medium bowl, whisk together the mascarpone cheese and double cream. Pour into the egg yolk mixture and whisk again, until combined.
3. In a separate bowl, whisk 2 of the egg whites, until they can hold stiff peaks. Fold them into the mascarpone/egg yolk mixture.
4. Fold the chopped candied fruit.
5. Arrange the sliced fruitcake on a plate and sprinkle the cherry liqueur over it.
6. Line a 1.5-quart loaf tin with plastic wrap. Arrange 2 slices of cake in a single layer in the base of the tin.
7. Pour half of the semifreddo mixture on top of the fruitcake. Arrange another 2 slices of fruitcake on top, followed by a layer of the remaining semifreddo and finish with a final layer of fruitcake.
8. Freeze for 5-6 hours.
9. When ready to serve, use the plastic wrap to help turn the semifreddo out of the tin, slice thickly and serve immediately.

(39)_Dried Cranberry, Pistachio, and Ginger Cannoli

Cannoli are an integral part of Sicilian cuisine; these tube-shaped pastry shells get filled with a sweet ricotta stuffing and passed around at important celebrations, and family get-togethers. During the Feast of the Seven Fishes, the classic cannoli often gets a holiday makeover. In this recipe, festive dried cranberries, chopped pistachios, and crystallized ginger are used to jazz up this Italian classic.

Serving Size: 25
Preparation Time: 15mins
Cook Time: N/A
Total Cooking Time: 5hours 15mins
Ingredient List:

- 4 cups ricotta cheese
- 1 cup mascarpone cheese
- 2 cups confectioner's sugar
- 1 tablespoon orange peel (grated)

- ½ teaspoons vanilla essence
- ¾ cup crystallized ginger (minced)
- ¾ cup tart dried cranberries (minced)
- 4 ounces semisweet choc chips
- 25 cannoli shells
- Pistachios (finely chopped)
- Confectioner's sugar (for dusting)

Methods:
1. Into a food processor, add the cheeses, sugar, orange peel, and vanilla essence. Blitz until smooth.
2. Add in the crystallized ginger and dried cranberries and pulse until well incorporated and finely chopped.
3. Add the choc chips and pulse a few times until incorporated.
4. Transfer the filling to a pastry bag (with no tip) and refrigerate for an hour.
5. Pipe the chilled filling into the cannoli shells and dip the ends in chopped pistachios.
6. Arrange on a cookie sheet or plate and refrigerate for 3-4 hours.
7. Dust with a little confectioner's sugar before serving.

(40)_Double Chocolate Rum Stuffed Panettone - Panettone Ripieno al Doppio Cioccolato

Food historians believe the baking of panettone dates back to the Middle Ages. However, it's precise origin is hotly debated with many legends and stories laying claim to its invention. This light and fluffy bread is popular worldwide with many Italian families buying panettone loaves in bulk to give as gifts to friends and family. If you find yourself with a box of this delicious fruit studded bread, then why not brush it with rum, stuff it with white chocolate and serve as a heavenly dessert.

Serving Size: 6
Preparation Time: 5mins
Cook Time: 15mins
Total Cooking Time: 20mins
Ingredient List:

- 1⅓ cups double cream (divided)

- 5⅓ ounces white chocolate (chopped)
- 5⅓ ounces dark chocolate (chopped)
- 1-pound whole panettone
- 1¾ ounce white sugar
- 2 tablespoons rum

Methods:
1. In a saucepan warm half of the cream, taking care not to boil.
2. Add the white chocolate and stir gently until it melts.
3. Repeat the process in a clean saucepan with the remaining cream and dark chocolate.
4. Set both melted chocolates aside for a moment.
5. Slice the panettone into 5 horizontal slices and set aside.
6. To make the syrup, add the white sugar and just under half a cup of water into a saucepan.
7. Heat, while stirring, until the sugar has dissolved. Take off the heat and set aside to cool.
8. Stir the rum into the cooled syrup.
9. Use a pastry brush to cover each slice of panettone with the rum syrup.
10. Put the panettone back together, using the white chocolate as 'glue' to hold the slices together.
11. Spread the dark chocolate over the entire outside of the panettone and set aside until entirely set.
12. Slice and serve!

Appetizers

When you're waiting at a restaurant for your food to get out, it might take a while. Depending on how packed the restaurant is and how long your food usually takes will determine how long you have to wait. An appetizer can give you something to eat while you wait for your main course.

The best things about appetizers is that they can be a huge variety of things. While you don't have to have gourmet appetizers, there are still plenty of things to make that won't take a whole lot of time, but will keep your family and friends happy.

Tomato-Mozzarella Bites

10 min, makes 20, 58 calories

These are a quick and easy appetizer that can be made the morning of your big get-together. All you need for this appetizer is some skewers, mozzarella, and tomatoes, along with a few other ingredients. This is a healthy and delicious appetizer to keep your guests ready for the big meal.

Ingredients
2 tbsp. olive oil
2 tbsp. white Balsamic Vinegar
¼ tsp. oregano
¼ tsp. each salt and pepper

20 grape tomatoes
40 basil leaves
20 mini mozzarella balls
Directions:
1. Whisk olive oil, white balsamic vinegar, oregano, salt, and pepper in a large bowl.
2. Add the mozzarella balls into the mixture and toss, coating them evenly.
3. Put onto the skewers, alternating between the mozzarella, tomatoes, and basil. There should be one mozzarella ball, one tomato, and two basil leaves on each skewer.

Stuffed Mushrooms

45 min, makes 20, 67 calories, 350F, 177C

These are always a wonderful treat and can be made up to three days in advance. If you have a lot of people coming over, this is a great appetizer/snack for them to enjoy while the main course is being made.

Ingredients
20 medium white mushrooms
1 tbsp. unsalted butter
2 tbsp. olive oil
½ small onion
½ small green pepper
Black pepper
1 clove of garlic
2 tbsp. lemon juice

1 can of minced clams
¼ cup chopped flat-leaf parsley
¾ cup bread crumbs
¼ cup grated parmesan
¼ cup coarsely grated mozzarella
Directions:

1. Set the oven to 350F.

2. Take the mushrooms and take off all the stems. Finely chop the stems, they will be used in the stuffing.

3. Heat a skillet on medium, putting the butter and 1 tbsp. olive oil inside. Add onion, green pepper, and black pepper. Cover for 4 minutes, stirring occasionally.

4. Add mushroom stems and garlic, stirring for 2 to 3 minutes. Stir in clams for 1 minute.

5. Remove your skillet from the heat and let it cool for 5 minutes. Stir in the lemon juice, bread crumbs, parsley, and both kinds of cheese.

6. Toss the mushrooms in the remaining olive oil. Place them on a baking sheet with the stem hole facing up. Divide the mixture between all of the mushrooms, or approximately a spoonful each.

7. Cook in the oven until golden brown, 20-25 minutes.

Homemade Salsa

20 min, 12 servings, 34 calories

Salsa and chips is a great appetizer, even before a big dinner like Thanksgiving. It's perfect for watching the football game while dinner cooks and is nutritious for being salsa.

Ingredients:

1 white onion, chopped
1-2 jalapenos, chopped (optional)
1 clove garlic, chopped
8 Roma tomatoes, chopped
1 can of diced tomatoes
1 can of green chilies
1 handful of cilantro
1 tbsp. lime juice
1 packet of Stevia
¼ tsp. sea salt

Directions:

1. Chop all the ingredients.
2. Add everything to a food processor and pulse. For a chunky salsa, pulse until just combined. For smoother salsa, continue pulsing until desired thickness.
3. Put a bag of your favorite chips in a big bowl and serve!

Snacks

Like with the appetizers, snacks will help keep your guests from grumbling about the food. These are also good after the festivities of the day. As it gets later, their stomachs are sure to start rumbling again. If you have grand plans for the leftover turkey and don't want them touching it, make some of these snacks for them instead.

Cheese and Crackers Platter

10 min, 190 Calories

Who doesn't love cheese and crackers? They are the perfect thing to serve as a snack or an appetizer to your guests. It's quick and easy to make and will keep them pretty happy.

For this, you'll need to choose what kinds of crackers and cheese you'll want to serve, making this recipe very versatile. Here is a basic platter you can make:

Ingredients:

2 boxes of Simply Balanced Multigrain Crackers
20 slices of goat cheese
20 slices of muenster cheese
20 slices of pepper jack cheese
20 slices Monterey jack cheese

Directions:

1. Slice up all the cheese.
2. Arrange the crackers and cheese on a tray in any way you would like and serve!

www.ingramcontent.com/pod-product-compliance
Lightning Source LLC
Chambersburg PA
CBHW072010070526
44583CB00015B/1416